THE
Essential Oil Maker's
HANDBOOK

THE
Essential Oil Maker's
HANDBOOK

Extracting, Distilling & Enjoying Plant Essences

Bettina Malle & Helge Schmickl
Translated by Paul Lehmann

Spikehorn Press
Austin, Texas

The Essential Oil Maker's Handbook

Copyright © 2015, Bettina Malle and Helge Schmickl

All rights reserved. No part of this book may be used or reproduced without written permission except in cases of brief quotations embodied in articles and books.

Although the author and publisher have made every effort to ensure that the information in this book was correct at press time, the author and publisher do not assume and hereby disclaim any liability to any party for any loss, damage, or disruption caused by errors or omissions, whether such errors or omissions result from negligence, accident, or any other cause.

Spikehorn Press
4029 Guadalupe St.
Austin, Texas 78751 U.S.A.
512-220-0544
mailbox@spikehornpress.com • *www.spikehornpress.com*

Printed in China

Originally published as Ätherische Öle selbst herstellen
©Verlag die Werkstatt, 2012
Front cover photography © tanjichica7/iStock/Thinkstock
Back cover photography © Marilyn Barbone/iStock/Thinkstock
Interior photograph credits © Thinkstock xii, 4, 17, 18, 63, 64, 95, 96, 116, 117, 118, 121, 122, 129, 130, 133, 136

Publisher's Cataloging-in-Publication
Malle, Bettina.
 [Ätherische Öle selbst herstellen. English]
  The essential oil maker's handbook : extracting, distilling & enjoying
    plant essences / by Bettina Malle & Helge Schmickl ; translated
    by Paul Lehmann. — English-language edition.
  pages cm
  Includes index.
  LCCN 2015933315
  ISBN 978-1-943015-00-9
  ISBN 978-1-943015-01-6 (ebook)
  1. Essences and essential oils—Amateurs' manuals. I. Schmickl, Helge.
II. Lehmann, Paul (Translator), translator. III. Translation of: Malle, Bettina.
Ätherische Öle selbst herstellen. IV. Title.

TP958.M27513   2015   661'.806
                          QBI15-600051

Contents

Preface to the English-Language Edition — vii
Preface to the First Edition — ix
Introduction — xi

1. Historical Overview — 1
2. Basics — 5
3. Making Your Own Oil, Step by Step — 19
4. Distillable Materials — 65
5. Using Your Oils — 97
6. Frequently Asked Questions — 123

Afterword — 131
Harvest Calendar — 134
Index — 137
About the Authors — 143

Preface to the English-Language Edition

Although the German-language version of this text is currently available in a fully revised fifth edition, we felt like another revision was due for the first English-language edition of *The Essential Oil Maker's Handbook*. In addition to converting all metric units into U.S. customary units, we've also added the many new facts and experiences that we've collected in the years since last revising the German edition. Our knowledge on the subject has grown much more than we first thought; as we read through the text nearly every topic brought to mind new ideas and information that demanded to be told. Especially with hydrosols—there has been a series of rapid developments in this field since the last revised edition. Some sources even call the use of hydrosols in health care the "new aromatherapy." Nine years ago the focus was on essential oils; hydrosols were commonly considered a nice but less-than-valuable by-product. This opinion has changed radically. Nowadays lots of home producers are *only* interested in hydrosols and consider essential oils a pleasant by-product. These producers nevertheless confirm what has been our experience: the most intense hydrosols are obtained only if everything is done to get the maximum essential oil yield.

In this edition, we have included even stronger descriptions of the basic conditions needed to maximize the oil yield, not only concerning the preparation of the plant material but also the appropriate still construction and distilling procedure. We discovered that, especially with small stills, construction is crucial to determining whether essential oil can be received in great amounts or not at all.

In former editions we mainly described the uses of the essential oils; now there are as many recipes for hydrosols as essential oils in fields as varying as health, cosmetics, cleaning, cooking, cocktails, etc.

If you're interested in producing your own essential oils and hydrosols on a small scale (e.g., for home use) you will find here detailed and easy-to-follow instructions to obtain those valuable products and plenty of descriptions of how to use them.

We wish you great success!
Dr. Bettina Malle and Dr. Helge Schmickl

Preface to the First Edition

There are many magazines and books that provide information on how essential oils work and how they're used, but there's essentially nothing on producing essential oils in small quantities as a hobbyist. Doing so is actually easier than you might think, as long as you have the proper know-how. This state of affairs inspired us to make our experience in this area from our seminars on aromatic oils, among other sources, available to the broader public. This book is a practical handbook and, along with the basics of the theory of use, is above all intended to show you how to actually make the oils.

When we first became interested in essential oils, we originally just wanted to find a use for the herbs, flowers, shrubs, and trees in our garden rather than simply composting the leftover portions of the plants as we had been doing up to that point. We immediately thought of producing essential oils as we already knew the methods, at least in theory, from our studies of chemical engineering. Over time, this interest developed into a very fascinating hobby, and we became passionate collectors of homemade oils. To supply the base materials we needed, we planted herbs and flowers in addition to the plants that we already had available, and we also collected parts of coniferous trees when we went for walks and occasionally even pruned our neighbors' bushes. Bit by bit, these plants become a distillate, but unfortunately our still was not suitable for making oils. We had to develop a new apparatus that was designed keeping in mind the specific issues that arise when distilling this sort of material at the quantities we needed. After a few failures, we slowly began to see positive results; each distillation and each plant provided us with new experience. We also wanted to use the oils that we produced for bodily care so that we could also learn something about their effect on the human body. Although our initial creams were too solid and our first shower gel barely foamed at all, we were finally able to find the proper formulas. We're now happy to provide you with the sum of our experiences.

We wish to express our gratitude to the participants in our seminars and the visitors to our website who contributed to this book through their many tips and suggestions.

We hope that you enjoy this practical handbook. May it serve as a starting point for your many future successes.

Good luck!
Dr. Bettina Malle and Dr. Helge Schmickl

Introduction

Demand for essential oils has increased so sharply in recent years that shortages are not an infrequent occurrence. At times, certain oils are very difficult or completely impossible to acquire in their pure forms. Since oil merchants deal in large quantities—2.2 pounds (1 kilogram) of rose or lemon balm oil costs about U.S.$7,000 (€5,000)—it's very tempting for vendors to produce the oils artificially. Modern production methods make it difficult for consumers to tell the difference between an original and a copy, and only the most precise methods of analysis can do so with accuracy.

If you want to be certain that the oils and hydrosols you're using are natural and free of chemicals, it's very simple to make them yourself, an art that has long been all but forgotten. Essential oils are produced almost exclusively in large commercial operations nowadays, and hydrosols are mostly still considered an unwanted by-product. This book will allow the distillation of herbs, blossoms, roots, and branches to become a hobby that's once again accessible to anyone.

After a brief look at the history and the necessary background knowledge, chapter 3 provides step-by-step instructions on how to produce your own oils and high-grade hydrosols. How does the oil-making equipment work? How do you make it yourself? How are oils and hydrosols distilled? How can you separate a mixture of oil and hydrosol?

The next chapter lists all the important domestic and exotic base materials from which oils and hydrosols can be made, with detailed information on what part of the plant to use, when to harvest, the effects of the plant, and what ailments the different plants are generally used against.

Chapter 5 covers the uses for essential oils and hydrosols. In this chapter, you'll find the core recipes for perfumes, body oils and creams, bath oils, shampoos, soaps, etc., as well as liqueurs.

We conclude the book with some frequently asked questions. They may prove an important aid if you encounter certain potential issues.

After reading this book, you will be able to build a suitable apparatus and produce these excellent oils and hydrosols yourself as well as to make and use a wide variety of products from them.

We hope your efforts are enjoyable and successful!

CHAPTER 1

Historical Overview

Essential oils have been used for their medicinal properties and fragrances for at least five thousand years. But resin and wood were already being burned long before that, in the Stone Age, as a form of offering to the gods. Almost every ancient culture smoked dried plants, grasses, resins, fruits, and bark. They were used for cleaning, as offerings, and to treat illnesses. Fragrant ointments made from mashed blossoms were sometimes also used as cosmetics or to alleviate various maladies.

In ancient Egypt, essential oils were used to heal wounds or to help prevent inflammation. They distilled turpentine, cedar, and cinnamon and dissolved oils from blossoms in fatty oils. Egyptian priests used this method to produce incense cones, ointments, and powder. Essential oils made from resin and plants played an important role in Egyptian burial practices. The bodies of the dead were prepared by covering them with melted resin from coniferous trees, which had a disinfecting effect. The cloths used to wrap up the mummies were soaked in disinfecting incense and myrrh. Aside from medicinal and religious uses, essential oils were also used by the people as perfumes or deodorants. The Egyptians mixed myrrh, thyme, and rosemary with fat and rubbed it onto their bodies. The more expensive pure oils were reserved for the pharaohs. Vases containing fragrances were found in King Tut's tomb—they hadn't lost any of their aroma after three thousand years!

Old essential oil still with worm and essencier ▼

The ancient Hebrews, Sumerians, Assyrians, and Chinese were also all aware of smoking and the usages of fragrant plant essences. In Ayurveda in ancient India, essential oils were already being used medicinally, but the emphasis was on massages with sandalwood.

The ancient Greeks developed stills, which were then adopted by the Romans, and perfected the use of oils in baths. Rome's fragrant baths allowed it to become the "bath capital of the world" by the time of Jesus. Perfumes and fragrant body oils were also created there at this time.

The Arabs later improved on the earlier distillation methods, allowing them to extract especially strong essences. This made them the world's foremost producers of premium fragrances. The Persian doctor Avicenna (980–1037) improved what was then the common method of producing plant essences, which allowed pure essential oil to be extracted.

In the Middle Ages, especially in the monasteries of Europe, there was an extensive body of knowledge about how to produce essential oils and their healing powers. Among other causes, the countless religious wars ensured that this knowledge ended up being largely lost.

In the sixteenth century, the doctor Paracelsus (1493–1541) investigated the relationships between essential oils, plants, and their ingredients. Around the same time the doctor Hieronymus Brunschwig wrote a book about distillation.

The English doctor and astrologer Nicholas Culpeper (1616–1654) greatly expanded popular awareness of essential oils' uses in healing. His writings on the healing and stimulating powers of herbs and plants influenced many European alchemists, healers, and doctors.

▲ Old essential oil still with cooling dome at the Musée International de la Parfumerie (Grasse, France)

Beginning in the mid-nineteenth century, especially in France, the effects of essential oils on the human body were first investigated scientifically. At the beginning of the twentieth century, the French chemist René-Maurice Gattefossé started experimenting with perfumes and cosmetics. He recorded his discoveries about the healing abilities of various plants in the book *Aromatherapy*. This is still the common term for treatment using fragrant plant extracts. Due to the general public's increasing interest in alterna-

Historical Overview

◂ Essential oil still with worm, storage tank for perfume maturation in the background (with fluted paper filter and filtration container)

tive natural healing methods, herbal medicine and aromatherapy have now been firmly incorporated into natural healing.

Nowadays, any exotic fragrance can be synthesized in a test tube. This development has made the fragrances widely affordable, and underlies the clear trends in the industry. In 1960, about 40 percent of fragrances were produced naturally. That figure dropped to 15 percent by 1980 and to just 8 percent by 1995 as the tendency toward synthetic fragrances continues. True essential oils, however, are pure, natural products that cannot be synthetically imitated due to their countless ingredients and many active substances and fragrances.

◂ Old stills used to distill lavender oil

CHAPTER 2

Basics

This chapter will take a brief side trip into chemistry and teach you what essential oils and hydrosols actually are, how they can be used, and the difference between them and artificial products. Then you will be given an overview of the different methods of producing aromatic oils and information on how to check their quality.

What are essential oils and hydrosols?

Essential oils

The term "essential oil" generally refers to an aromatic substance that originates from a plant. If you smell a flower, herb, or spice, you're perceiving the scent of the essential oil. You can find essential oils in different parts of the plant, for example:

Leaves: Sage, eucalyptus, rosemary
Blossoms: Rose, jasmine
Peels: Lemon, orange
Wood: Sandalwood, cedarwood
Roots: Valerian, ginger
Bark: Cinnamon bark
Resin: Myrrh

Natural essential oils are always made up of a large number of chemical compounds whose combination gives the oil its fragrance and healing power. They are exclusively made up of volatile components and predominantly contain monoterpenoids, monoterpenes, sesquiterpenoids, sesquiterpenes, aldehydes, alcohols, esters, ethers, and ketones.

Nowadays, almost all fragrances are also made synthetically. However, doing so never reproduces all of the substances that characterize the particular oil, but generally just the smell, which is just one single component. So even if you can perceive the smell of a synthetic lavender fragrance, for example, it will not contain any healing properties.

True essential oil	Fragrance and healing properties
Artificial oils	Fragrance only, no healing properties

Essential oils are not fatty oils. If you drip a drop of it onto a piece of paper and then let it dry, no grease stain will be left behind, though some color may be if the oil is colored. In contrast, cooking oil, for example, is fatty and would leave a grease stain on the paper.

Essential oils don't mix with water, so they can be extracted via steam distillation (see chapter 3). They are soluble in high-proof alcohol, fatty oils, milk, and honey, among other substances. Organic solvents such as hexane, ether, and carbon tetrachloride can also dissolve the oil very well.

Hydrosols

Because essential oils don't mix with water, the distillate of an herbal steam distillation consists of both an aqueous and an oil layer. The aqueous layer goes by many names, including hydrosol, hydrolate, herbal distillate, floral water, herbal water, and essential water. We have decided to use the most popular term, hydrosol. Hydrosol contains distillable water-soluble components and is often a colloidal suspension (this is the meaning of "hydrosol" in the chemical sense, a cloudy colloidal suspension of oil and water) of essential oils too.

In the past, hydrosols were often considered a by-product of distillation, but now they are an important coproduct. Aside from flavorings, they are also used for medicine, cosmetics, health care applications, cooking, baking, drinks, and plenty of other household applications. Some sources even call their use in health care the "new aromatherapy."

All instructions for maximizing the essential oil yield (see chapter 4) are crucial for hydrosols also. If the maximum possible oil yield is received, the hydrosol will be the most intense.

Extracts

Many books on herbs repeatedly talk about plant and herb extracts. Plant extracts do contain essential oils, but the proportion is too small to separate out the oil from them. Extracts are therefore used directly in this form. We differentiate between two different types of extract.

Aqueous extracts	For aqueous extracts, the plants are placed in water (without heating it), decocted, or added to boiling water like when preparing tea. These extracts contain practically zero essential oils because water can only very poorly dissolve these parts of the plant.
Alcoholic or oily extracts	If the plant is pickled in 96 percent ABV ethanol (drinking alcohol), for example, a tincture will appear. (Cooking) oil is used for oily extracts. In both variants, the essential oil is dissolved in the

liquid, but the content is not high enough to then extract the essential oil from it (see extraction process for more information).

You've surely noticed that there are usually multiple varieties of a given type of essential oil. This is because a plant will produce oil with different characteristics depending on what region it comes from. For example, the altitude that the plant grows at is crucial.

If essential oils are used for medicinal purposes, the scientific (Latin) name of the plant is always important. There are about a hundred different plants called "eucalyptus," but their effects differ. Only the scientific name can exactly specify the proper plant.

There are three different ways of making fragrances used in perfumes and other products: natural, synthetic, and artificial. A natural fragrance refers to an essential oil from a plant. Synthetic fragrances or aromas are imitations of natural fragrances made in a laboratory setting. An artificial fragrance is also created in a lab, but doesn't exist in nature at all.

For the sake of completeness, we will also explain the term "essence," which is often lumped together with essential oils but really refers to something else. An essence is a synthetically produced product. Its base materials can be either natural or artificial components. A "100% natural essence" thus refers to a synthetically produced product whose base materials were natural. These products are generally used in the food sector.

"Essential oils" are often offered for sale from plants that don't contain any essential oils at all. They're just artificial fragrances. Well-known examples include lily of the valley, lilac, and apple oils. Edible fruits do not generally contain any essential oils.

The term "spagyric" is often used in connection with essential oils. This word probably derives from two Greek roots: "spao" (to separate) and "ageiro" (to unite, to join). Spagyric essences are produced by first separating the active ingredients from the plants being used by means of an elaborate process, then working with them and finally recombining it all again.

Uses

Essential oils and hydrosols can be used in a wide variety of ways in our everyday lives, spanning from health to maintenance to well-being to cooking (more details in chapter 5). Their most important uses are:

Essential oils and hydrosols develop their fragrances especially well in warm water and are absorbed both through the olfactory nerves and through the skin.

Different varieties of the same species are called chemotypes.

Example:
– Thyme linalool
– Thyme geraniol

Thyme indicates the species and linalool and geraniol the chemotypes making up these two different oils.

Example:
100 percent natural spike lavender essence:
No real spike lavender has ever come near this product. It's made from natural camphor, natural linalool, and natural terpenes.

Aroma baths

Flavoring	Many essential oils and hydrosols can be used to flavor food and drinks. Spicy oils should be diluted in cold-pressed vegetable oil so they can be added in reasonable dosages. Herbs such as basil, ginger, caraway, marjoram, or oregano work especially well as flavoring oils. Hydrosols are dilutable with water, hence they can be mixed with mineral water, all kind of soft drinks, or alcoholic beverages.
Skin care	The fragrant essences in facial creams, lotions, and gauze pads improve our well-being. The active ingredients of the naturally pure essential oils or hydrosols are absorbed by the skin and spread by the circulatory system.
Fragrant oil burners	A fragrant oil burner helps you easily create a pleasant living environment. A tealight under the cup heats up the mixture (water and a few drops of essential oil) or pure hydrosol, allowing the fine fragrance to spread. Some oils/hydrosols have a slight disinfectant effect, which can be especially helpful during the flu season.
Hair care	With the help of essential oils and hydrosols, you can make your own special shampoos and hair tonics that are especially helpful for issues like dandruff. These problems can often be alleviated by the effects of the oil/hydrosol alone, without having to add any chemicals.
Internal uses	Unless you have special subject-specific knowledge, you should only use essential oils externally and heavily diluted (e.g., with gauze pads, nasal oils, by gargling water, etc.). It's also possible to ingest oils, of course, but this should only be done after consulting a doctor. Despite their nice smells, you must not forget that some of these substances are heavily toxic in their pure, essential oil forms. Pure, self-distilled hydrosols are much more intense than the ones available for purchase. In principle, it is possible to drink your self-distilled hydrosols pure, but it is advisable to catch up on the intake of hydrosols first.
Body and massage oils	Whether it's an oil to improve athletic performance or for a partner massage, aromatic skin oils can be used in a variety of different ways and can be prepared according to your own wishes. Cold-pressed vegetable oil works well as a base oil, as does jojoba oil, almond oil, macadamia oil, wheat germ oil, or avocado oil. The base oils include valuable nourishing ingredients that provide the skin with nutrients.

Basics

Liqueurs

Even today, many essential oils form an important part of professionally produced liqueurs because this is the only way for the producers to guarantee that the contents aren't being affected by seasonal fluctuations and that the quality and composition of their products always remain consistent.

If you make your own liqueurs, it's possible to use hydrosols instead of water.

Perfumes

Making your own perfumes and perfume oil mixtures is an interesting and exciting challenge. The most surprising thing about it is that many people who have an allergic reaction to store-bought perfumes don't react at all to homemade perfumes from homemade oils.

Extraction methods

How can the volatile essential oil be extracted from the plant in a highly concentrated form? We will now give you a brief overview of the various possibilities, which will be described in greater detail in chapter 3.

Steam distillation

The simplest and gentlest method of extraction is steam distillation. Hot steam is led through the chopped-up plants in a container, which carries the volatile oils along as well. After the subsequent cooling of the steam, you get both the essential oil and the hydrosol (water-soluble components as well as a colloidal suspension of essential oil in some cases). In principle, you can use this method to produce oil from almost any product. A significant advantage of this simple method is that many environmental toxins and pollutants are not volatile and therefore cannot make it into the oil. Pesticides, however, which are very frequently used in plant cultivation, can rarely be 100 percent removed. You should therefore always be sure to at least check that your base materials are high-quality, untreated, organically grown plants; otherwise the oil will not benefit your health but do the opposite.

Some producers boil the plant parts directly in water rather than extracting from them with steam. This

Hydrosol: water with a small amount of oil, water-soluble components, and a colloidal suspension of essential oil

Steam still ▼

The Essential Oil Maker's Handbook

▲ Old still for fractional distillation

method has the disadvantage of overcooking a large proportion of the temperature-sensitive substances, which has a strong negative effect on the quality of the oil.

Fractional distillation

The composition of the distillate (the liquid that drips out of the condenser) changes over the course of the distillation. The most volatile components appear first, while those with a higher boiling point don't appear until later. If the receiver container for the distillate is switched out multiple times during distillation, you'll end up with several fractions of the distillate, each with a slightly different composition. This is referred to as fractional distillation.

In a conventional still, where the steam is led along the shortest possible route from the kettle to the condenser and then cooled, this method only makes sense under certain conditions. The individual components are not separated completely enough, causing each fraction to contain more or less everything; the components are just concentrated. If the "concentrated" fraction goes through fractional distillation a second time, the components in the new fraction will be concentrated even further, etc. You can avoid this very labor-intensive, continual distilling if your still has a vertical reflux column (essentially a column with a series of built-in fixtures and packing material) between the kettle and the condenser. Inside this column, the rising steam partially condenses (becomes a liquid) and then evaporates again, condenses again, etc. By the time it's reached the very top of the column, the steam will have been distilled many times consecutively. How many times depends on the construction and height of the column.

Modern reflux stills with columns for fractional distillation ▼

A reflux still therefore allows more precise separation than a conventional one. In principle it's nothing more than a normal distillation carried out many times consecutively. This more precise separation makes it even possible to separate individual components of an essential oil's fragrance. For example, fractional distillation allows you to separate the rose fragrance from geranium oil or the camphor from lavender.

In general, use a still without a column to steam distill plant materials in order to receive as many different volatile substances as possible. The resulting essential oils and hydrosols contain a broad variety of active components, making them valuable for uses like aromatherapy. The pharmaceutical industry only needs one specific active pharmaceutical ingredient (API), therefore the raw oil is distilled again, this time with a reflux column and under vacuum because the water vapor is missing. Steam has the ability to extract components from the plant material that have a higher boiling temperature than the steam temperature (100°C or 212°F). A vacuum is therefore needed when distilling pure essential oils without water vapor because it lowers the boiling temperature of liquids. The disadvantage of a vacuum device, if you're not using liquid nitrogen as cooling medium, is the loss of highly volatile components; the vacuum pump sucks them out.

Co-distillation
Some plants only release their fragrance if they're distilled along with a carrier that absorbs the fragrance. The carrier is usually another plant that contains oil, or sometimes even an essential oil directly. Typical co-distilled oils include (young) stinging nettle leaves, aromatic hay, and algae. Cedar or rubber trees are usually used as plant-based carriers, though copaiba balsam, a syrupy liquid extracted by scratching the bark of certain types of copaifera, is also used.

In many of these combinations, the fragrant plant and the carrier are coordinated with each other (e.g. meadowsweet with rosemary, lemon balm with lemongrass, chamomile with lemon oil, or orange blossoms with bergamot oil).

Cold pressing
This method of extracting essential oils is suitable only for citrus fruits, whose peels are chopped up and mixed with a little water. After the pressing, the essential oil is separated from the aqueous phase in a centrifuge.

Cold pressed essential oils also contain waxes and resins, therefore they are colored and opaque. Whether this is an advantage or disadvantage depends on the use of the oil. On the one hand, many believe that citrus oils should be pressed because citrus aromas are temperature sensitive. On the other hand, citrus oils contain a phototoxic substance, so sunbathing after applying a cold-pressed citrus massage oil to the skin is not recommended. This problem doesn't occur with steam-distilled, clear, and colorless citrus oils, which emit a pleasant citrus scent, too, by the way.

Extraction method
In this method, the oil is separated from the plant with the help of an extracting agent (i.e., it is extracted). We distinguish between the following types depending on the extracting agent.

Solvent extraction

The plant parts are heated along with organic solvents such as hexane, petroleum ether, or carbon tetrachloride. When industrial quantities are made this way, the finely chopped plants are placed on grates stacked on top of each other, and the solvent flows through level by level. Since essential oils are very soluble in these solvents, almost all of the oil can be extracted this way. The solvent is then evaporated and recycled using vacuum distillation. A solid, waxy, fragrant mass is left behind as residue, the so-called *concrete*, a base material. The concrete can be used for soap production, but this mass is usually just an intermediate step in essential oil production.

The concrete is usually heated along with ethanol in the next step. The residue left over after the alcohol has evaporated is called the *absolute*, which unlike the concrete is a tough oil (i.e., a liquid).

Solvent extraction results in considerably higher yields than steam distillation, but a (very) small amount of the solvent is always left behind. This remnant makes the oil unsuitable for medicinal or aromatherapeutic uses.

Another drawback to solvent extraction: all the solvents used belong to the benzene, petroleum ether, and alcohol groups. But some components of essential oils are also alcohols in the chemical sense. Due to the variety of substances that essential oils can be made of and their chemical similarity to solvents, mixtures and compounds can form that nobody can exactly predict, recognize, or identify, let alone detect during the residue check. All that is checked for then is the chemical presence of the original solvent, which under these circumstances will have been reduced to an undetectably low level. However, you will not be able to quantita-

Example:
You can get about 8.8 ounces (250 grams) of essential oil from 1.1 short tons (1,000 kilograms) of roses, but 5.5 pounds (2.5 kilograms) of concrete or 3.3 pounds (1.5 kilograms) of absolute.

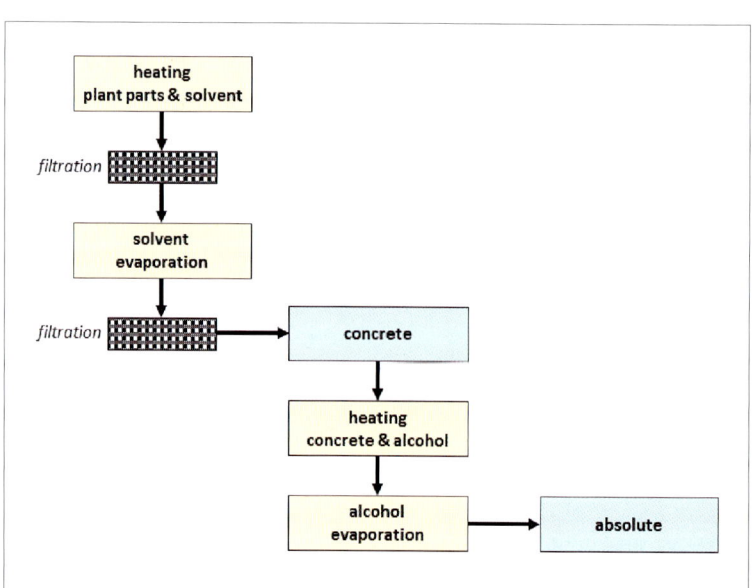

Solvent extraction diagram ▶

Basics

▲ Rose concrete (left) and rose absolute

tively or qualitatively assess what new, possibly stable compounds have arisen during the process.

Enfleurage

In this process, blossoms of plants such as jasmine or roses are placed in lard (other fats can also be used instead, see chapter 3), allowing the fat to extract the fragrant substances. After one to two days, the blossoms should be replaced with new ones and the process should be repeated until the fat is saturated with the fragrance,

◀ Enfleurage with blossoms

which takes about two to three months. The oil-containing fat is called *pomade*. Alcohol is then poured over the lard, which dissolves a large portion of the oils in the alcohol. Then the alcohol is evaporated or the alcoholic solutions are used directly. Enfleurage is almost only ever used for demonstrative purposes nowadays.

Maceration/Infusion

Maceration* is the oldest method of oil extraction. It works similarly to enfleurage, but the plants are infused in a neutral carrier oil (see chapters 3 and 5). The plants are switched out repeatedly until the carrier oil is saturated with essential oil. To accelerate this process the oil is often heated to 149°F (65°C). The concentrated oil can either be used directly or treated with alcohol like in enfleurage.

Resinoid process

This method is most useful for extracting oil from resin. The resin is heated with toluene or ethanol. The essential oil dissolves relatively well in it, but it's still necessary to boil the mixture for hours or even days. The solvents then evaporate. Since it's not possible to completely remove the solvents in this method either, it's preferable to use ethanol as the solvent.

Carbon dioxide extraction

Carbon dioxide and/or butane, which liquefy under pressure, dissolve the essential oil from the plant. Oils that are made in this manner have a different composition from oils extracted with steam. It's not yet clear whether this leads to any drawbacks when using them in aromatherapy.

Checking the quality

Just as long as the history of essential oils is the history of fakes! Along with many chemical analysis methods, there are several methods of physical analysis you can use to check the quality of an essential oil: color measurement, density measurement, measuring the refractive index and the boiling and melting points, etc.

A modern method is to analyze the composition and quantitative distribution of an essential oil's components. The various components can be separated using gas chromatography and then analyzed. Chiral gas chromatography is the most useful, in which the individual enantiomers are separated in the oil. This is the only method that allows you to recognize whether a substance is of synthetic or natural origin. Enantiomers are molecules that are mirror images of each other. Their layout is the same, but they cannot be

---

* In German the word "Mazeration" means unheated infused oil, whereas "Infusion" refers to warm maceration. This distinction is not necessarily made in the English usage of these terms, however.

▲ You can only be certain your essential oil isn't fake by making it yourself.

superimposed over each other. As far as their chemical behavior goes, enantiomers are like two completely different substances, and they are also physically different to a large extent.

What can you conclude from this? Nature produces compounds with different enantiomer ratios than laboratory chemists. This means, for example, that more "right" molecules would be present than "left" molecules in a real oil. If this oil is re-created in a lab, however, it will have more "left" molecules than "right" molecules. This allows you to tell how natural an oil really is from a gas chromatogram. This is especially important in aromatherapy because oils with a "natural enantiomer ratio" have a completely different effect on the body than synthetic oils with a different enantiomer ratio.

In 1989, an experiment demonstrated that about 80 percent of commercially available lavender oils were fake. Discovering this would have been impossible without chiral gas chromatography.

The most recent development in testing the authenticity of essential oils is crystallography. This method is even reliable in cases where chiral gas chromatography cannot deliver meaningful results because crystal growth and geometry are so specific that even oils from the same type of plant but originating from different places can be distinguished.

Synthetic fakes aren't the only ones out there, however. Expensive essential oils are often mixed with cheaper ones, such as vervain with lemongrass, lavender with lavender hybrids, or rose

Note: Fake synthetic versions of the following oils are often seen: bergamot, lavender, lemon balm, rose, jasmine, geranium, cinnamon, neroli, petitgrain, mountain pine, rosemary, thyme.

with geranium. It's also common to dilute true essential oils with neutral oils and/or paraffin oil. This is the most common (because it's the cheapest) forgery method nowadays, as it is with perfumes, but fakes of this type can be detected with the simple "grease stain test" (see page 6). Since raw oils are usually only available in an impure or adulterated or diluted form, they're always purified via reflux distillation before they're used. How exactly this purification is carried out depends on what the end product is being used for. For pharmaceutical products, the oil must be purified very thoroughly, whereas a medium amount of purification is enough for cosmetic products and soaps, and oils for fragrant oil burners are often sold unpurified.

The term "essential oil" is not currently legally protected, meaning that "pure essential oil" appearing on a bottle does not necessarily guarantee that it really contains a true, naturally pure essential oil.

CHAPTER 3

Making Your Own Oil, Step by Step

The few available sources on making your own essential oils at home imply that doing so is a complicated process. However, with a little bit of effort, you can make your own oils very easily. An herb garden is certainly helpful, but many products, such as citrus fruits and spices, can be found at any supermarket. We will now explain exactly how easy it is to produce all-natural essential oils using the processes just described.

Steam distillation

Steam distillation is a very gentle method for distilling any plant. Oil can even be extracted from citrus fruits using this method. The resulting essential oil is free of chemicals—as long as you've used clean plants—and can unhesitatingly be used in any sort of product.

The principle

What is meant by the terms distillation and steam distillation? In a distillation, a mixture of two or more liquids is brought to a boil, producing steam. This steam has a high concentration of whichever component of the mixture has the lowest boiling point. The steam is then led into a condenser where it is condensed via cooling, turning it back into a liquid. This product, the so-called distillate, now has a higher concentration of the substance with the lowest boiling point.

A classic application of distilling is the production of liquor. Here, we distill fermented fruit or grain, basically an alcohol-water mixture with a low alcohol content. Water boils at 212°F (100°C) and alcohol (ethanol) at 173.3°F (78.5°C), which causes the steam to have a higher concentration of alcohol. The product is a high-proof alcohol, or rather brandy.

In **steam distillation**, the substance being distilled is not placed directly into the water, but rather above the boiling water. The steam carries the volatile substances along with it and flows along with them to the condenser, where the mixture condenses again.

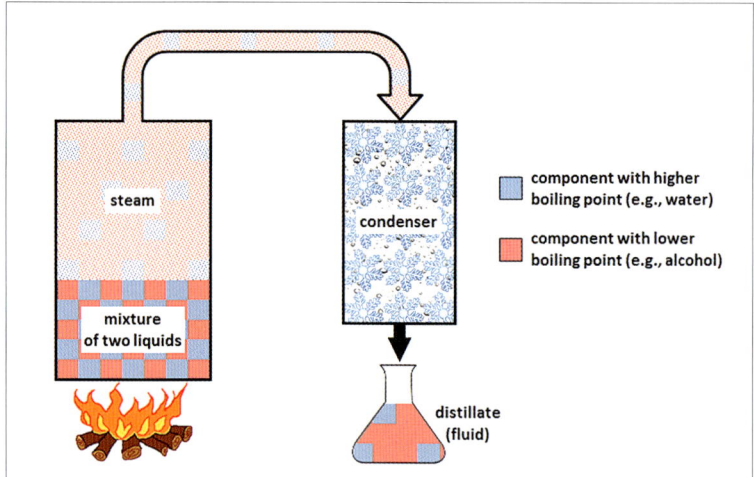

Schematic chart of distillation ▶

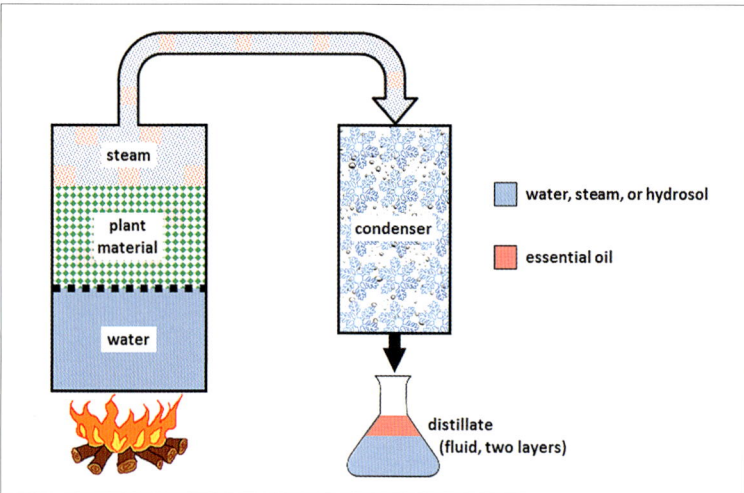

Schematic chart of steam distillation ▶

After the cooling, the distillate will be a liquid, just like in normal distillation. However, the liquid water and the liquid essential oil do not mix with each other, but rather form two layers: the oil layer, which except for a few exceptional cases always floats on the top, and the watery layer, which is almost always found at the bottom. The watery layer is called the hydrosol, hydrolate, floral water, or herbal distillate and has an essential oil content of up to about 5–8 percent.

You're surely familiar with situations where two liquid layers are present from cooking: if you make a salad dressing from vinegar and oil, the oil floats on top.

The hydrosol is made up predominantly of the water-soluble ingredients of the plant, which were brought along by the steam, while the oil contains the fat-soluble ingredients.

Making Your Own Oil, Step by Step

Stills

To make your own essential oils according to the principle just described, you'll need a still. Stills are made up of a **kettle**, which contains both the water and the substance that you're distilling (the plant parts you want to extract oil from). The kettle is fitted with a **steamer basket**, a kind of sieve that holds the substance that you're distilling above the water. This allows it to be placed in the steam chamber without being overcooked. The still also needs a **heat source**. This can be a gas burner, a spirit lamp, an electric stovetop, a gas stovetop, or even an open fire. If the water in the kettle is heated to a boil, steam will form. The steam climbs upward, permeates the substance you're distilling, and carries the essential oils from the plant with it. The upper portion of the kettle will contain both water and essential oil in the form of steam at this point.

The kettle is sealed in an airtight manner with the **still-head**, a type of cover, so that no steam can leak out. The still is certainly not completely sealed, however, as the top of the still-head is fitted with a pipe, called the **lyne arm**. The lyne arm carries the steam to the worm in the condenser. The **condenser** is a sort of pot filled with cold water that washes around the worm—a spiral-shaped pipe inside the pot—and cools it. The steam is cooled in the worm until it condenses (i.e., becomes a liquid).

◂ Two layers, using signet marigold (see page 81) as an example: above, the oil layer (signet marigold oil), below, the aqueous layer (signet marigold hydrosol)

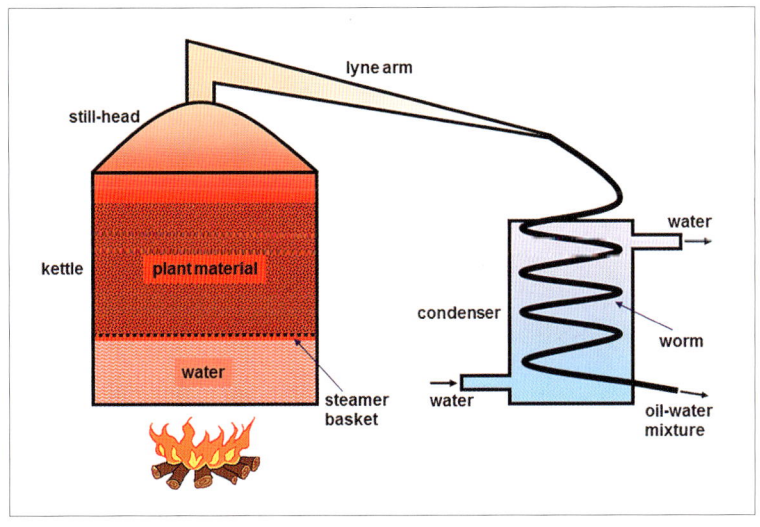

◂ Structure of steam distillation

Building your own still

There are multiple approaches to building your own still. They range from professional stills to simple devices that can be found in any kitchen. You have the following options for constructing a still:

The Essential Oil Maker's Handbook

Simple designs:
- Tea kettle
- Pressure cooker
- Wok still

Professional designs:
- Classic still with a lyne arm
- Classic still with a vertical condenser
- Glass still

Tea kettle

This option is a very appropriate choice for your first attempt.

Take a tea kettle and fill it half full with water. Then add the finely chopped plant material into it. If the kettle has a lid that doesn't close airtight, seal it with a Teflon tape (PTFE thread sealant tape, available at hardware stores). Seal the mouth of the kettle (after removing the valve) with a stopper with a hole. Insert a 2-inch (5-centimeter) glass pipe into the hole in the stopper and attach an approximately 3-feet (1-meter) silicone hose that leads to a glass bottle. The bottle must not be sealed airtight with the hose. Make sure that the hose is always pointed downward from the kettle all the way to the bottle or else liquid will collect in it. Don't use a rubber hose because the water-oil mixture in the form of steam can take on the smell of rubber very quickly.

Heat the tea kettle. As soon as the water begins to boil, steam will begin to escape through the mouth. In this simple design, the piece of hose serves as the (air) condenser, so the steam must condense while still in the hose; only liquid may leave it, no steam. If the piece of hose isn't long enough for this to occur, double the

Materials list:
- Tea kettle
- About 3 feet (1 meter) of silicone hose that fits with the glass pipe
- Stopper, with a hole for the glass pipe (chemical resistant, ideally silicone)
- 2-inch (5-centimeter) glass pipe
- Glass container (e.g., a small bottle)

Cost: about U.S.$40 (€30)

Example:
If you fill the kettle with 1 quart (1 liter) of water, you should distill until there is about 20 fluid ounces (600 milliliters) in the receiver container.

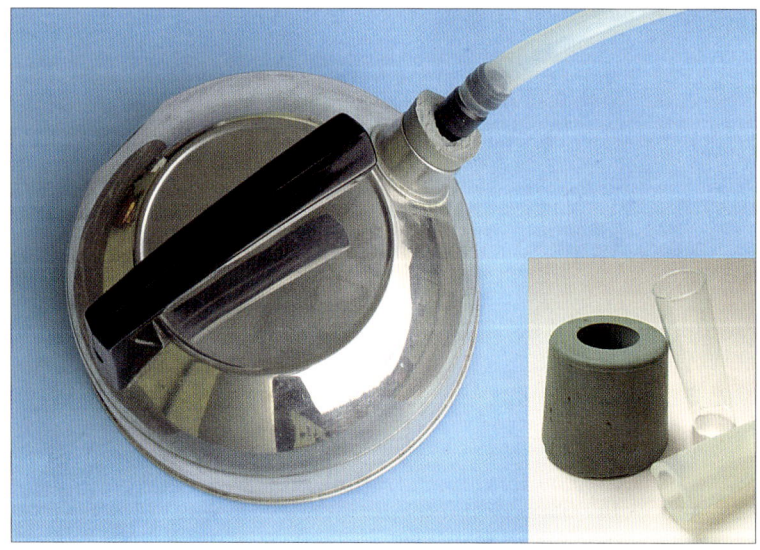

Tea kettle with stopper, glass pipe, and silicone hose ▶

Making Your Own Oil, Step by Step

length by using a tube clip and another 3-feet (1-meter) silicone hose, and wrap a cold, wet cloth around it. Switch the cloth out as soon as it gets warm.

You can end the distillation process once two-thirds of the volume of the water that you poured into the kettle has collected in the bottle.

The final product is a strongly fragrant water—but you can't expect a high yield of essential oil. The plant material is overcooked in the teapot, which destroys some of the aroma, so you don't get as high-quality a product as with a true still. You can use the fragrant water directly in place of the hydrosol in some products (see chapter 5).

Advantages:
+ Very easy to build
+ Very appropriate for a first attempt

Disadvantages:
− You get very little essential oil, just fragrant water
− The plant material is overcooked because there's no steamer basket
− The condenser is ineffective and only condenses part of the steam

◂ Pressure cooker with stopper, glass pipe, and silicone hose

Materials list:
- Pressure cooker
- Steamer basket (e.g., steaming attachment, pasta strainer, metal sieve)
- 2-inch (5-centimeter) glass pipe
- Stopper with a hole for the glass pipe (chemical resistant, ideally silicone)
- About 3 feet (1 meter) of silicone hose that fits with the glass pipe
- Glass container (e.g., a small bottle)

Cost: about U.S.$150 (€110)

Pressure cooker

Extracting oil with a pressure cooker works similarly to doing so with a teapot. However, in this case you have the option of incorporating a steamer basket, which raises the quality of your product by keeping the plant material from being overcooked.

The steamer basket should not reach all the way to the bottom; it should stand on feet. This keeps the plant parts in the steam

23

The Essential Oil Maker's Handbook

▲ Metal sieve

Steamer basket with extension tubes ▶

chamber rather than in the water. Steamer inserts from the hardware store work well, but the feet have to be lengthened with small metal pipes, sold by the yard or meter at hardware stores. If the inner diameter is a bit larger than the feet, squeeze the pipes with a pair of pliers to the desired diameter. A metal sieve also works well, but make sure the feet are long enough.

The distillation process works the same way as with a tea kettle. Pour water into the pressure cooker—the water level should remain beneath the bottom of the steamer basket. Then add the plant material. Remove the overpressure plug and seal the nozzle with a plug with a glass tube inside it like in the tea kettle method, and stick the hose into the glass tube. You should also only distill until you have two-thirds of the volume of the water you poured into the kettle to ensure that the kettle never becomes completely empty while it's still being heated. Be sure to use a continuously descending cooling hose that's further cooled with a damp cloth if necessary.

This method also results in a product that is mostly fragrant water or rather hydrosol. The quality is significantly better, however, because the plants are not overcooked.

Advantages:	+ Very easy to build
	+ Very appropriate for a first attempt
Disadvantages:	− You get very little essential oil, just hydrosol
	− The condenser is ineffective and only condenses part of the steam

Making Your Own Oil, Step by Step

Wok still

This very simple design comes closest to being a true still because it incorporates water cooling so that most of the steam actually condenses.

Materials list:
- Large cooking pot
- Steamer basket
- Wok
- Cup made of heat-resistant glass, ceramics, or metal

Cost: about U.S.$165 (€120)

Take a pot, as big as possible, and fill it with water up to just beneath the bottom of the steamer basket. The steamer basket should be the same as described in the previous example. Before you actually add the plants, place a cup in the middle of the basket. Next, spread the plants around the cup such that the inside remains empty. Now place the wok on the pot. The wok has the benefit of being rounded underneath and not having a flat bottom, which is the only way for the condensate to collect at one location. Check that the deepest part of the wok is directly above the cup and fill the wok with cold water. As soon as the water in the pot is boiling, the steam will rise and be cooled on the underside of the wok. The condensed steam (the distillate) will then drip from the middle of the wok—the deepest part—into the cup underneath. End the distillation once the cup is almost full. If the cooling water in the wok heats up, scoop some of it out and replace it with cold water (ideally along with crushed ice).

▲ Structure of a wok still

This still design is almost perfect. The only disadvantage is that the distillate collects *inside* the kettle, causing it to be heated during the entire distilling process, which diminishes the quality of the oils somewhat.

◀ Wok still

Advantages: + Very easy to build
+ Very appropriate for a first attempt
Disadvantages: − The distillate is hot during the distillation
− You can't see whether the receiver container is full yet
− You can't use a bottle with a narrow neck as a receiver container, which makes it harder to transfer the essential oil later

Materials list:
- Large pot with a cover that can be sealed airtight (e.g., a pressure cooker)
- Steamer basket: wire mesh, about 10 inches (25 centimeters) squared, with a metal ring with feet underneath that it fits to
- Column: copper pipe, diameter: 0.8 inches (2 centimeters), length: 2 inches (5 centimeters)
- Angled reducer from 0.8 inches (2 centimeters) to 0.4 inches (1 centimeter)
- Lyne arm: copper pipe, diameter: 0.4 inches (1 centimeter), length: 1.3 feet (40 centimeters)
- Copper reducer from 0.4 inches (1 centimeter) to 0.2 inches (0.5 centimeters)
- Condenser: copper pipe, diameter: 0.2 inches (0.5 centimeters), length: 10 feet (3 meters)
- Round wood or bottle
- Cooling container: plastic bucket

Cost: about U.S.$200 (€150)

Classic still with a lyne arm

This type of still has a professional design. The still works without pressure and includes a condenser. The kettle can be made out of a variety of materials: copper, stainless steel, aluminum, or glass. The kettle needs a wide opening so that the steamer basket can fit into it. If you can't find a suitable insert, you can also easily make one yourself: build a metal hoop with approximately the same diameter as the kettle. Attach three feet to the hoop. Then place metal fly screen from the hardware store across the hoop. Make sure that the basket doesn't fit too snugly in the kettle or it may be difficult to remove after the distillation is finished.

The kettle's cover can be flat or curved. It must be possible to seal the cover onto the kettle in an airtight manner. Don't use rubber for this seal, just silicone or Teflon. You can also cut a silicone hose lengthwise and use it as a seal. Or use a mixture of flour and water. This mixture hardens when heated, so simply smear it over the leaky area.

The lyne arm should lead from the middle of the cover, which should also be the highest point, to the condenser at a gentle downward incline. Using a lyne arm that leads vertically upward would leave behind many components of the essential oil.

To keep an excessively high pressure from building up in the kettle when it's boiling, the lyne arm's diameter should be about 1 inch (2.5 centimeters) for a still with a kettle volume of up to 2 gallons (8 liters).

The lyne arm carries the distillate to the condenser, of which the simplest type to build is the worm condenser. To make one, you wrap a narrow copper pipe or something similar with an interior diameter of about 0.2 inches (0.5 centimeters) for a still with a kettle volume of up to 2 gallons (8 liters) around a round piece of wood, a bottle, etc. For stills of up to 2 gallons (8 liters), the worm should be about 5 feet (1.5 meter) long, with about 1 inch (2.5 centimeters) of space between loops of the spiral. The worm is built into a pot or bucket to facilitate water cooling. If you furnish the cooling pot or bucket with two nozzles, one for cold water to flow in (at the bottom of the pot) and one for cooling water to

Making Your Own Oil, Step by Step

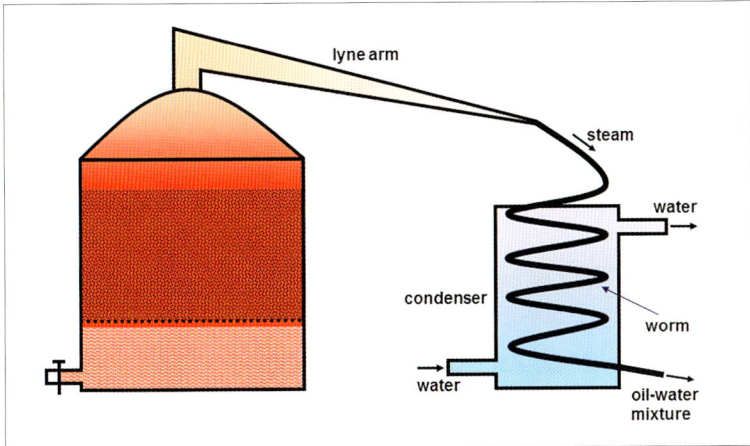

Note: The still should be constructed in a way that allows it to work without any pressure buildup, which damages the aromas and is dangerous.

◂ Still with lyne arm and worm condenser

flow out (at the top of the pot), you can connect the condenser to a water line. Make another hole in the bucket for the distillate's outflow valve and seal it with sanitary silicone.

An alternative to the worm condenser is the Liebig condenser (named for its inventor). A Liebig condenser makes use of an enclosed straight pipe attached to the kettle-lid or lyne arm at a gentle downward incline—thus the steam inlet is on the top. The steam condenses on the inside. The enclosure is fitted with two valves, one for cooling water to flow in and the other for it to flow out. If you choose to use this kind of condenser, it should be attached at a gentle downward inclination. Make sure that the cooling water flows through the enclosure in an upward direction.

A significant advantage of the Liebig condenser when distilling essential oils is that oil cannot get caught in the condenser's spirals. It's also easy to clean with a thin bottle brush.

To remove essential oils residues from a spiral or a long Liebig condenser, clean it with alcohol (i.e., ethanol; food-safe alcohol, not denatured alcohol or methanol!) or acetone. If using alcohol, the alcohol content must be at least 80 percent ABV (alcohol

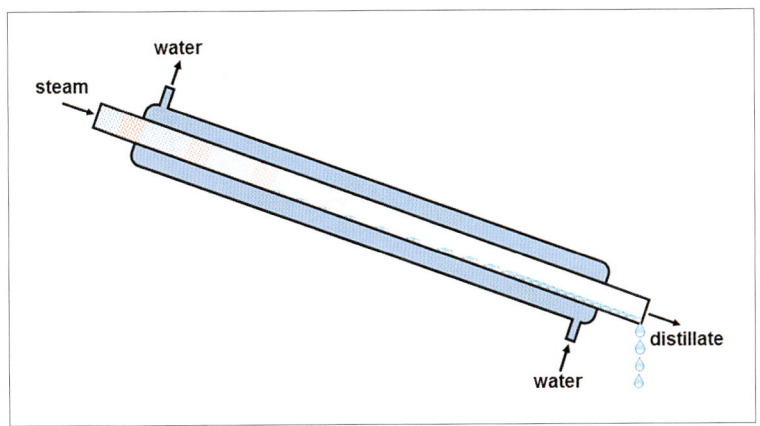

◂ Liebig condenser

Materials list
- Large pot with a cover that can be sealed in an airtight manner (e.g., pressure cooker)
- Steamer basket: wire mesh, about 25 centimeters squared, with a metal ring with feet underneath that it fits to
- Glass condenser with NS 24/29 ground glass joint
- Metal tube, diameter: 1 inch (3 centimeters), length: 1 inch (3 centimeters), with external threads and a matching screw nut

Cost: about U.S.$480 (€350)

by volume). Clean the worm by filling it halfway with alcohol or acetone, shaking it vigorously, emptying out the liquid, and, particularly in the case of acetone, thoroughly rinsing it out with dishwashing liquid and warm water first and then with warm water only.

Advantages:	+ Excellent cooling
	+ No column, so oil yields are optimal
	+ Plant material in the steam chamber
Disadvantages:	– Lots of effort to build
	– Oil losses if you use a worm condenser

Classic still with a vertical condenser

It's also possible, of course, to mount the condenser directly above the kettle. In this case, the steam flows directly into the condenser after it leaves the kettle. A reflux condenser is suitable for this type of design, in which the distillate trickles downward against the rising current of steam. The picture below shows a version that includes an integrated column. Inside the condenser is a vertical pipe through which the steam reaches its upper third. The cooling water flows through a worm that is wrapped around this pipe. The steam condenses on this worm and flows downward in the cooler, toward the drain for the distillate.

The column causes a reflux effect (see "fractional distillation" section) which separates some components of the essential oil, keeping them from making it into the distillate. Another disadvantage is that some of the oil gets caught in the spiral, which is especially irritating when you're working with plants that produce low oil yields. As with any other condenser, you can wash this oil out of the condenser with alcohol after distillation is finished so that you at least have it in an alcohol solution.

Reflux condensers are made of heat-resistant glass and are available from laboratory supply vendors. You'll need an adapter if your kettle is made of metal. You can use a metal pipe with a somewhat larger diameter than the lower condenser nozzle. The pipe is attached to the kettle cover with a nut. The condenser is attached to the top and the gap between the metal and the glass is sealed with heat-resistant (257°F or 125°C) sanitary silicone.

Vertical condenser with integrated column ▼

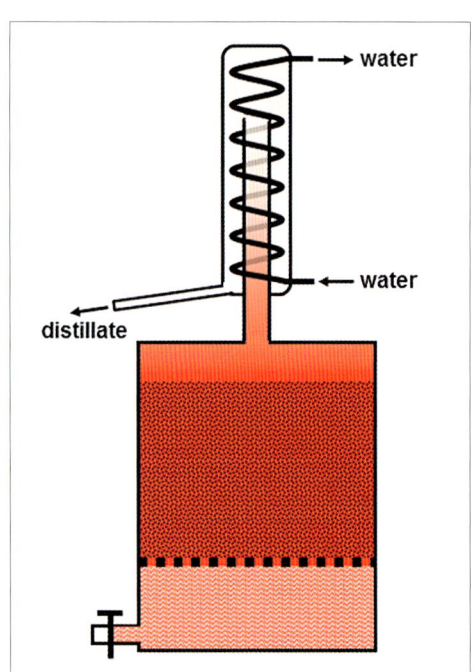

Making Your Own Oil, Step by Step

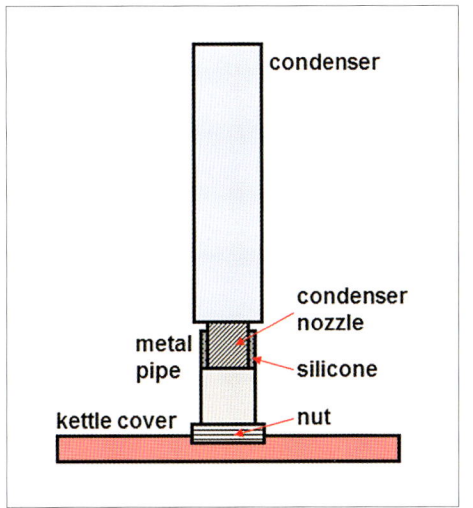

▲ Metal-glass adapter fitting for reflux condenser

▲ Kettle with reflux condenser

Advantages:	+ Perfect cooling
	+ Plant material in the steam chamber
Disadvantages:	− Lots of effort to build
	− Some loss of aroma due to the long vertical steam pipe
	− Oil losses in the spiral

Glass still

A still can also be built out of the right laboratory equipment because glass parts can be connected to each other in a gas-tight manner using ground glass joints. Not all equipment is suitable for our purposes, however. A round-bottom flask, for example, cannot be used as a kettle because its opening is too narrow to fit in a steamer basket. You can, however, use the flask as a steam generator and connect a pipe between the flask and condenser, or a flask filled with plant material with two ground glass joints at the top and the bottom.

Electrical heating can be accomplished with a heating mantle, the shape of which fits well with a round-bottom flask.

A steam generator also offers another possibility. It is a pot or flask in which water is brought to a boil. You could also use a tea kettle instead. As the steam leaves the pot, it's led through a pipe (or flask with two openings) filled with plant material and then cooled back down. A receiver container should be placed under the pipe with the plant material because a substantial amount of water condenses on it, especially at the beginning while the apparatus is still cold. You can also use silicone hoses to conduct the steam.

Materials list:
- Round-bottom 5-liter flask, NS 24/29 ground glass joint
- Glass pipe with joints on both sides, NS 24/29 ground glass joints
- Condenser with NS 24/29 ground glass joint
- Heating mantle or oil bath

Cost: about U.S.$520 (€380)

Advantages: + Excellent still
Disadvantages: – The water that condenses at the beginning also contains oil, which is then not in the distillate

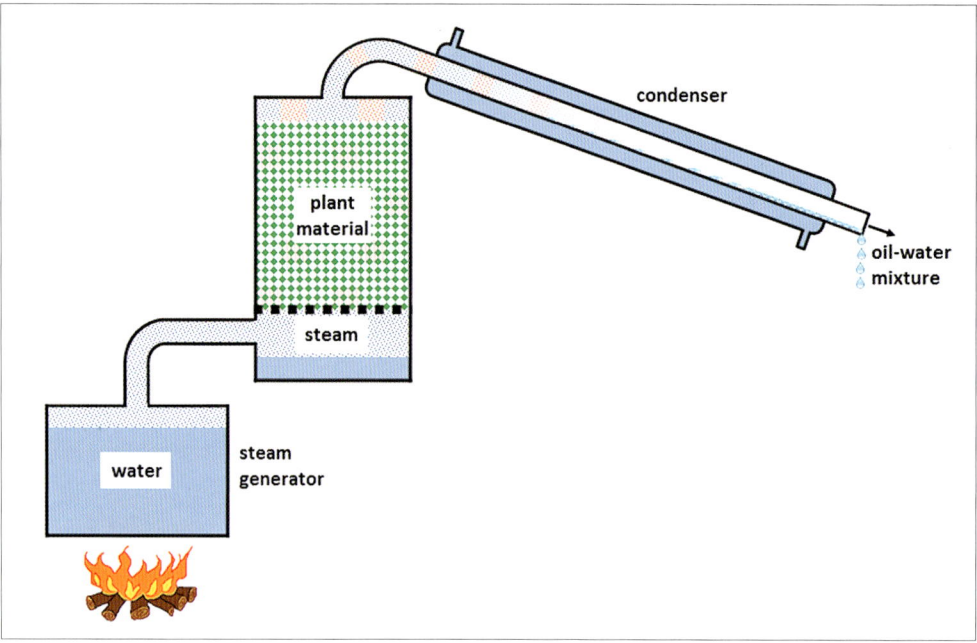

▲ Still with steam generator

Buying a still

If you're considering buying a still for oil distillation, you should be sure to consider the following points so that it will deliver your desired results:

1. The still must contain a steamer basket or else there's no sense in using it for steam distillation. Oil should only be extracted from the herbs and blossoms by *steam*, not by them floating in the water.
2. Make sure that the kettle has a wide opening for adding and removing plant material and that your kettle is large enough that your oil yield won't be too low.
3. The pipe that carries the steam should be as wide as possible. The thinner and longer this pipe is, the higher the pressure drop will be in the still. The consequence of this is a certain pressure buildup in the kettle. Even a small pressure buildup can cause the steam temperature to rise, destroying some of the aroma.
4. The material that the still is made of must not affect the aroma of the steam or the liquid. For example, you should avoid rubber seals that aren't chemical resistant because they'll make the oil smell like rubber. Heat-resistant glass, stainless steel,

or copper are ideal materials as none of the three affect your final product.

5. The still must be fitted with a powerful burner or the bottom of the kettle must be suitable for a stovetop. Otherwise, the distillation will take too long, especially the heating, and the aromas in the kettle will be destroyed.
6. The still should absolutely not be set up to automatically recirculate the hydrosol back into the kettle for several reasons, not only because the hydrosol can't be collected in this case (see page 51).
7. The following point mainly applies to beginners: make use of professional advice, because you're sure to run into many questions at the beginning of your journey into "oil artistry."

Small stills

The ideal still for producing essential oils from a technical standpoint would stick to the principles that Leonardo da Vinci was already following in his sketch. They include no (unnecessary) steam conduits or columns after the kettle, as these can have a negative effect on the diversity and quality of the distillate ingredients. The condenser is located directly above the plant material—the steam is therefore cooled back down immediately after absorbing the oil. The less time the volatile components spend exposed to high temperatures, the better the quality of the essential oil will be. A dome that is cooled from above serves as the condenser, which ensures that there are no losses within the still. Then the distillate is led along the shortest possible path to the receiving container. This type of still is thus perfect for smaller quantities and for plants that provide a very low oil yield.

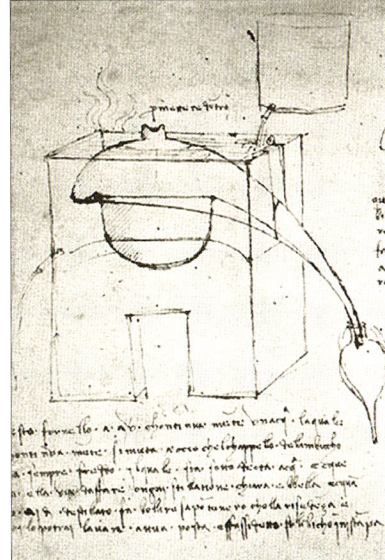

▲ Leonardo da Vinci's original sketch

We developed and constructed the Leonardo Classic and Leonardo Grande stills* according to these principles. These handcrafted stills are made of beaten copper, a material denser, harder, and more resistant to chemicals than common copper. Verdigris, a well-known problem with untreated copper, doesn't occur in these stills with normal use. The still consists of three parts aside from the steamer basket. In both versions the lowest part, the waterkettle, has a size of 0.5 gallons (2 liters) to ensure that it meets legal limitations for water (steam) distillation in many countries, such as Austria, Switzerland, or the United States (every still with a kettle larger than a certain nationally defined volume must be registered at customs to prevent people from distilling alco-

---

* Cheap knockoffs of our Leonardo still abound, so be careful when making a purchase. Only our Leonardo is patent protected.

The Essential Oil Maker's Handbook

Leonardo Classic still with steamer basket filling volume:
- plant material 0.92 gallons (3.5 liters)
- water 0.5 gallons (2 liters)

Cost: about U.S.$600 (€448) ▶

hol without paying taxes). The middle part, the container for the chopped plant material, is not too thin or too high in shape, thus unwanted reflux effects are avoided. The same goes for its connecter to the condenser at the top—the diameter is wide enough. Experiments have shown that if this bottleneck is too narrow, no essential oil will form at all with stills of this size range. The Classic can be filled with 0.92 gallons (3.5 liters) of plant material, the Grande with 1.6 gallons (6.2 liters). To receive the maximal yield (amount of essential oil per pound [kilogram] plant material), the "empty" space between the contents and the condenser should be as small as possible, so it's best to operate a still filled to the maximum. We have thus constructed two different still sizes. The Classic has the absolute minimum filling volume to be able to separate essential oils if using "average" garden herbs. If for example 0.92 gallons (3.5 liters) of a certain material produce 3.5 milliliters of essential oil, almost no oil will form at all if using 0.5 gallons (2 liters) instead (an expected oil amount would be about 2 milliliters). The Grande is for plants with an extremely low essential oil content and for larger quantities of material. The third part, the dome condenser, is equipped with a water container large enough to effectively condense all of the formed steam. Filling and emptying of the plant material is easy without great effort. Because all inner parts of the still are accessible by hand, the entire still can be cleaned thoroughly with warm water and dishwashing liquid, using a cleaning sponge scourer and a tube cleaning brush for the distillate outlet.

Making Your Own Oil, Step by Step

◀ Leonardo Grande still with steamer basket
filling volume:
- plant material 1.6 gallons (6.2 liters)
- water 0.5 gallons (2 liters)

Cost: about U.S.$790 (€589)

Due to its simple handling, the highest yield of essential oil per pound (or kilogram) plant material compared to any other construction, and the very intensive hydrosols, the Leonardo is the preferred device among users in the fields of phyto-aromatherapy (herbal medicine/aromatherapy) and herbology in all German-speaking countries. Therapists, professional practitioners, pharmacists, perfumers, herbalists, herb nurseries, florists, herb/spice/tea merchants, research institutes, universities, colleges, and other educational services use the Leo as well as home users making their own cosmetic care products based on self-produced essential oils and hydrosols. Independently from us, several books from different authors were published in German describing using the Leonardo for the distillation of hydrosols and their use for cosmetic care applications, cooking, baking, drinks, and plenty of other household uses.

Other small essential oil stills have problems caused by small kettles/plant containers, narrow condenser connecters, condensers too small to efficiently cool the steam, inner parts that are not entirely accessible for cleaning, or intricate filling and emptying processes. Occasionally users of other small stills contact us because they are unable to separate oil with their stills, not even a drip. In one of these cases, we agreed to a kind of distilling competition between our still and the other one. He brought the plant material and his still and we ran both stills simultaneously, each filled with 3.3 pounds (1.5 kilograms) of finely chopped spruce needles. He received no oil, whereas our result was 1.5 milliliters of essential oil. Another person sent his Swiss pine needles to us, believing

Deluxe still 7.8 filling volume:
- total 2 gallons (7.8 liters)
- plant material 1.6 gallons (6.2 liters)
- water 0.4 gallons (1.6 liters)

Cost: about U.S.$760 (€565) ▶

they contained no essential oil. It was the same story: whereas his yield was zero, we received 7.5 milliliters from 4.4 pounds (2 kilograms) of needles.

The Leonardo can be obtained exclusively from our online shop or directly from us at home (see at the end of the book for address).

An example of a "conventional" type of still with a separate condenser and worm is the "Deluxe" still. We actually developed and constructed this device for distilling alcohol, to create brandies or spirits with a rich bouquet. Unlike with the dome-type of still, it is possible to distill alcohol with the Deluxe because a worm condenser is effective enough to condense the alcohol steam completely and the three alcoholic fractions—heads, hearts, and tails—can be separated using the mounted steam thermometer. The still has no column and its lyne arm runs downward at an incline, so it's a perfect pot still that can also be used to produce essential oils. The disadvantage is that a small portion of essential oil remains in the worm and can only be removed by washing it out with high-percentage alcohol. It is nevertheless a good alternative if you want to distill alcohol and produce essential oils with a single device.

The Deluxe can operate with several different kettle sizes: 0.5, 1, or 2 gallons (2, 3.8, or 7.8 liters). In the case of steam distillation, you should note that these values include the needed amount of water, which is 0.4 gallons (1.5 liters). Therefore, the most sensible size for a steam distillation is 2 gallons (7.8 liters). This kettle can be filled at most with 1.6 gallons (6.2 liters) of chopped plant material.

The Deluxe is also available exclusively at our online shop or directly at our house (see address at the end of the book).

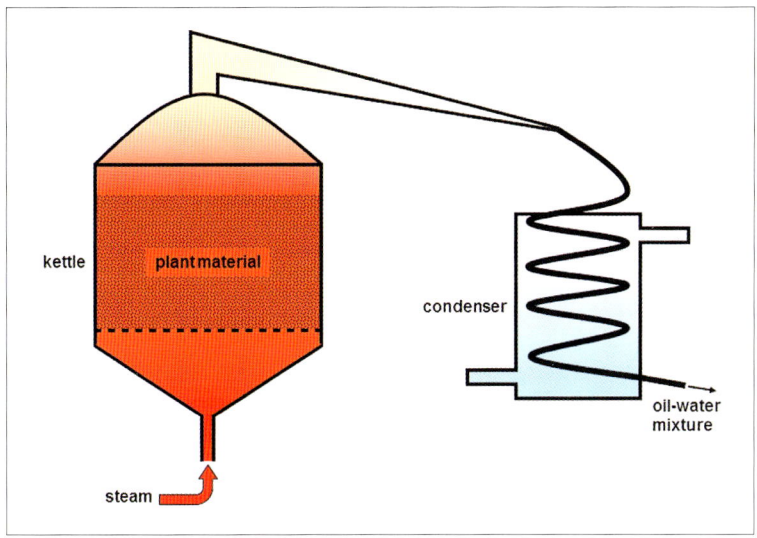

◀ Schematic chart of a large still with separate steam intake

◀ Rose oil production in Turkey

Large stills

In large stills, the steam is usually fed in from outside, meaning that the plant material never comes into contact with the boiling water. The image above shows a diagram of a still with a separate steam intake.

In Turkey, large copper stills are used to produce rose oil. Steam is also used to heat the roses in this case.

Preparing the plants

The oil yield depends both on when the plants are harvested and on how they're preserved and stored afterward (if they're not being used immediately). How small you chop up the plant before the distillation is also crucial. If you pay heed to all of these points, your result will be excellent.

Harvest

Roses and jasmine

Unfortunately, not all plants that contain essential oils can be harvested at the same time. Roses, for example, are harvested right after the flower heads have opened. The flower heads should be cut off shortly after sunrise after 5 a.m. and distilled immediately. This method is also common for other blossoms such as jasmine.

Rose picking in Turkey ▶

Lavender

Lavender, on the other hand, should not be cut before the blossoms start to wither. It's best to cut off about three quarters of the plant and let them hang drying upside down in small bundles for three days. With lavender, it's also possible to dry the plants for a longer time and distill them later. This is an especially good idea if you have a large amount of lavender. Make sure in this case that the plants dry out in a dry room with good airflow and no direct sunlight. After two to four weeks, the plants will be dry enough that they can be packed in an airtight container. In this stage it's easy to remove the dried blossoms from the stems if you want to distill the blossoms only, as professional lavender distillers do.

Herbs

With all herbs, you should wait for them to be in a late blooming stage, as with lavender (unless otherwise indicated in chapter 4), then harvest and distill them. The plants can also be hung upside down in bushels to dry and be distilled later. If you place the herbs in small open crates instead, you'll have to turn them over every day during the first week and make sure that the airflow is good. Otherwise, they'll start to get moldy. We unfortunately had this problem with the upside down bushels; they began to mold. For our next attempt we spread the (more or less uncut) herbs on several large sheets of packing paper, which we lay on the floor,

Making Your Own Oil, Step by Step

◂ Signet marigold, hung up to dry

not exposed to direct sunlight, in a room of about 68°F (20°C). During the first week we turned over the herbs every day, then twice a week for two weeks, and finally once a week. After one or two months the herbs were totally dried without any molding problems, and we could store them in paper bags. Because of the amazingly high oil yield when distilled, we now only dry our herbs this way. The herbs are dry enough once the leaves fall off with a crackle when they're touched, at which point the plants will have lost about two-thirds of their original weight. Then you should store the plants like tea, in cardboard boxes, paper bags or glass containers. Plastic bags such as freezer bags are not suitable for storing dried material because they dissolve the essential oils in it over time. You can also freeze fresh herbs—they're good for about eight months frozen.

> *Rules for drying herbs:*
> - Tie the herbs together in bundles and hang them upside down.
> - Dry them in a dark, well-ventilated, dry location.
> - The temperature must not exceed 86°F (30°C).
> - The drying will be finished after about two to four weeks (once the leaves fall off with a crackle when they're touched); don't leave them drying for any longer.
> - Store the herbs in dark conditions (e.g., in cardboard boxes, glasses, not in plastic bags).

Citrus fruits

It's important for citrus fruits to be distilled or pressed when they're fully ripe, not while they're still partly green. If you buy them from a store, you'll often run into the issue of them having been picked before they were ripe, which lowers your oil yield considerably. In this case, you can allow the fruit to after-ripen at home, but not too much. If the skin becomes thinner and leathery, the oil yield will drop down to a quarter of what it would be when fresh.

Seeds

Fully ripe seeds of spices like fennel or anise can be distilled fresh or dried (available from spice merchants).

Branches

It's best to collect branches of coniferous trees such as spruces, firs, or mountain pines between May and August. If you collect them earlier, the essential oils will only be present in very low concentrations. Unfortunately, drying them causes the oil to be lost.

> ☺ Tip: Branches can easily be stored frozen.

> *Rules that apply to all types of plant:*
> - You should only ever harvest a plant after at least three days of sunshine. This is when they contain the maximum possible oil concentration. Avoid harvesting after it rains or your yield will be low.
> - You should do something with the plant immediately after harvesting it—either chop it up and distill it right afterward or dry or freeze it. Otherwise, the plant parts will begin to ferment, destroying the essential oils entirely. Fermentation can begin after as little as thirty minutes—the inside of the bunch of clippings will get warm. Putting them in a cool place will delay the start of fermentation.

Cutting up the plants

Before distilling, the plants should be chopped up. We once cut thin mountain pine branches to a length of about 1 inch (2–3 centimeters) and distilled them. The result was essentially zero oil. We didn't let it discourage us and cut the branches to a length of about 0.1 inches (0.3–0.5 centimeters) the next time—an extremely laborious task if done by hand. But it was worth it—the oil dripped right out. It's also worth noting that we used the same material in both cases, and the branches were harvested and distilled on the same day.

Citrus fruits

There are two ways to work with citrus fruits. One is to cut them in half and press out the juice. You can drink the juice; it's not needed to produce the oil. Cut up the peels with a pair of scissors

Making Your Own Oil, Step by Step

◂ Oranges, pressed with a citrus juicer and chopped up

◂ Orange peeled with a potato peeler

and then chop them up with a food chopper, cutter mixer, or food processor (see page 40). A second, more labor-intensive option is to peel the fruits with a potato peeler, as only the outer, nonwhite, thin peel contains oils. The inner, thick, white skin gives the fragrance a bitter undertone. Chop up the thin peel before distilling it as well. Using this method, the oil yield per pound (or kilogram) of plant material is much higher, of course, because the kettle is filled only with oil carriers—the thin skin.

Spice seeds

Spice seeds such as anise or caraway don't need to be cut up before distilling. However, it doesn't hurt to crush them a little with a mortar and pestle.

Dried herbs

If you're working with dried herbs and the leaves aren't too hard, like peppermint leaves for example, then it's enough to just crumble them with your hands. Dried bay leaves, on the other hand, are very solid. They should first be torn up some with your hands and then chopped up into pieces of about 0.1 inches (2–3 millimeters) with a food chopper, cutter mixer, or food processor.

 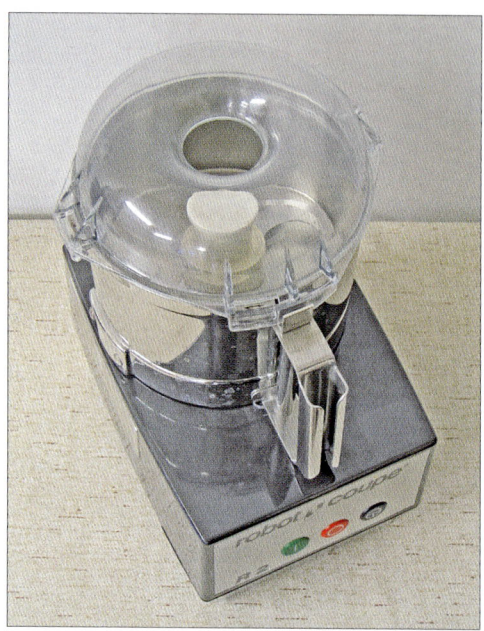

▲ A kitchen food chopper (above left) or professional cutter mixer (above right) is indispensable for preparing the plants.

Fresh herbs   Fresh herbs are usually used with their stems intact. First cut the plants to a length of about 1 inch (3 centimeters) and then chop them up with a food processor. A small household food processor doesn't work very well unless you've cut the herbs up with scissors first. After we used ours three times without preparing the herbs first, it started to smoke and stopped working.

Professional cutter mixers, a kind of robust food processor made of steel, do a much better job of cutting up and homogenizing vegetables, herbs, meat, etc. They're available in different sizes from about 1 to 2.5 gallons (3 to 9 liters) in specialty stores for restaurant equipment. These devices do cost more up front, but they're built so robustly that they can also chop up dried herbs, needles from conifers, seeds, and citrus peels without any issues.

Juniper berries   Juniper berries provide varying results depending on whether the berries are fresh or dried. As with other plants, your yield will be higher if you cut up the berries first. Dried berries give the oil a rougher, woodier character than fresh ones. Crushed juniper berries are available in stores. You can also crush whole berries with a mortar and pestle.

Bark   Hard bark such as cinnamon bark must be chopped up thoroughly or else the steam will only be able to reach its outer layers, leading to a low yield. Place the sticks of cinnamon in a dish towel and hit them with a hammer until the cinnamon is in small pieces (at most 0.5 by 0.5 millimeters).

Making Your Own Oil, Step by Step

◂ Whole juniper berries and crushed juniper

Petals

With very fine petals such as rose petals, it's enough to cut them up some with a pair of scissors.

Conifers

It's important to destroy the waxy layer coating conifer needles; otherwise nearly no oil will evaporate.

If you don't cut up small branches from coniferous trees or their cones enough, you'll get a correspondingly lower oil yield. You can use herb scissors with smaller amounts, and a garden shredder works well for larger amounts.

If you own a heavy-duty garden shredder, you can feed the chopped-up plant parts through a second time, this time with the current phase reversed. You couldn't chop it any more finely with a kitchen chopper.

▴ Garden shredder for cutting up branches

◂ Cinnamon can be broken up excellently with a dish towel and a hammer.

41

The Essential Oil Maker's Handbook

▲ Garden shredder, steps one (above) and two (below)

> ☺ Tip: If you're thinking about getting a new shredder, make sure that the blades cut both horizontally and vertically. This not only chops up the branches but also slices them open lengthwise so that the steam reaches their insides during distillation.

Plant	Chopping method
Citrus fruits	Scissors or potato peeler
Spice seeds (anise, caraway)	Don't chop, or crush lightly with mortar and pestle
Thin, dried herb leaves (peppermint)	Crumble by hand
More solid dried herbs (with thin branches, bay leaves)	First cut up manually and then use a food processor
Fresh herbs	First cut up with scissors, then use a food processor
Juniper berries	Crush with mortar and pestle
Hard bark (cinnamon)	Crush with a hammer
Petals (rose)	Cut up with scissors
Conifers (spruce, mountain pine)	Garden shredder

The distillation process

The following description may seem "trivial," but experience has shown us that distilling often produces no oil if the instructions aren't followed exactly. The most common mistakes are: wrong ratio of plant material to water, not enough plant material, excessively large receiver containers, receiver containers with the wrong shape, improper still construction, insufficient heating power, insufficiently chopped-up plants, improper handling or harvesting of the plant (see chapter 4), etc. If you fail to regard even seeming "trifles," this can seriously affect your yield. It's not just a matter of it being less than the expected amount—unfortunately, oil usually doesn't form at all in these cases. As far as quality and yield go among the small stills, the Leonardo has proven best for producing essential oils.

Before you start to work, you should always thoroughly clean the plant material. If you've previously distilled another type of oil, you can clean out traces of it from the still with some acetone or alcohol, then rinse it out well with warm water (although acetone and alcohol can dissolve essential oils, they mix very well with water). It's usually enough, however, to thoroughly wash the still with water and dish soap. If traces of a previous oil remain in the still, they will introduce impurities into your new product—just a few drops is enough.

Filling

First, pour tap water into the still. For kettle sizes of up to 2.1 gallons (8 liters), 6.3 cups (1.5 liters) is enough. If your still is larger, use 0.5–1 gallon (2–4 liters) of water. A rule of thumb: 2 cups of water per pound (1 liter of water per kilogram) of plant material. Be sure not to add too much water to the kettle or you'll see a reduced oil yield. Pay particular attention to this ratio when you're working with smaller amounts of material (less than 2 pounds or 1 kilogram). Using less water per pound (or kilogram) doesn't increase the yield any further, but it does create the risk of the still running dry since some plants, such as dried rosemary (page 86) or anise seeds (page 66), absorb some of the steam.

Insert the steamer basket. Make sure that the water level is beneath the basket.

If you're working with very finely chopped, almost powdery plants, like cinnamon, be aware that they can burn in the kettle in spite of the water due to some of the fine dust trickling through the steamer basket. In these cases, it's a good idea to place a paper towel or a cotton or linen cloth on the basket to keep the plant parts from falling to the bottom of the kettle and burning.

Once the steamer basket is in place, you can add the plant material. Be sure to weigh it first so that you can calculate the oil yield after the distillation (see page 53). Pour as much material in as possible. You can gently compress herbs, citrus fruits, blossoms, or branches in order to fit more into the still. The emphasis is on "gently"; pushing too hard can clog the still. If you're using seeds, you shouldn't push them because they collect densely enough on their own.

Very occasionally, the plant material you've added can quickly swell up into steam. This has only ever happened to us with a certain type of caraway and with well-chopped lemon peels. In these cases, you should only fill the still about three-fourths of the way full to keep it from clogging and its pieces from coming apart.

Rule of thumb: 1 quart (1 liter) of water per 2.2 pounds (1 kilogram) of plant material

> ☺ Tip: Yogurt cups filled with water and then frozen, crushed, and mixed with more water are great for cooling.

Filling the still

Fill the still with tap water ▶

◀ Insert the steamer basket and attach the middle part

Fill the basket with the herbs ▶

◀ Then attach the condenser

Fill it with cooling water ▶

◀ Place the receiver bottle under the still

Then the condenser is connected or attached. If you're adding the cooling water manually, you should fill the cooling container until it's overflowing and pour in more cold water as soon as the water has become hot. You can also use a crushed ice–water mixture or snow for cooling. Regardless of what kind of condenser you're using, if it continuously intakes cooling water (e.g., through a water line) the cold water should always run in at the bottom and the warm water should run out at the top.

Now you just need an appropriate receiver container for the distillate. The best option is small bottles that contain about 6.8-ounces (200 milliliters). You should make sure that the bottle has a long, narrow neck because the bottleneck is exactly where the oil collects. The narrower the neck is, the easier it will be for you to remove the finished oil. In a container with a wide opening such as a marmalade glass, on the other hand, the oil would spread across the entire surface, making it very hard to separate it from the hydrosol, especially if you get a low yield. Small, 6.8-fluid-ounce (0.2-liter) prosecco or piccolo champagne bottles have proven most appropriate. They have two further advantages: First, the flask narrows toward the top, so oil drops, which are lighter than water, will float upwards along the glass wall. An angle before the bottleneck would hinder this move. Second, the bottom is not flat but rather protruding upward in the middle. Therefore, it is easier to collect and draw off oils that are heavier than water because a narrow groove forms the deepest point of the bottle.

▲ Steamer basket with paper towel for very fine materials such as crushed cinnamon

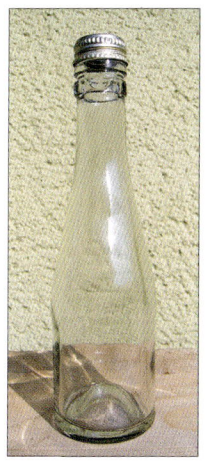

▲ Receiver bottle without an angle below the narrow neck to collect the oil and hydrosol mixture

Distilling

Once the still is constructed and filled, you can start the distilling process. Start by setting your heat source on maximum. It will take a while for the water in the kettle to start to boil; with an electric hot plate, it takes about ten to fifteen minutes for 1.5 quarts (1.5 liters) of water. It will take about that long again before the first drop of distillate appears because the steam has to permeate all of the plant material first. Starting as soon as the hydrosol-oil mixture begins to drip out of the condenser, check the temperature of the cooling water regularly.

You can continue to distill at your heat source's maximum setting. A 1,500-watt hot plate is enough for 1.5 quarts (1.5 liters) of water. At the optimal heating power, your distillate will be dripping out in a thin stream with short interruptions. If it's only coming out drop by drop, you need more heat.

In principle, the heating power can never be too strong, but you should make sure that the contents don't boil over. You can easily recognize this happening if, instead of the thin trickle or the rapid drops described before, an onrush of very cloudy, strongly colored water (somewhere from black-brown to a tea-like dark

Result of distilling dried and crushed oregano ▶

green depending on what's in the kettle, or a milky yellow with citrus fruits) suddenly comes out of the condenser at high pressure, possibly even along with some plant material. If this happens, immediately remove the still from the heat. Boiling over can also occur if a large amount of foam forms—this has only happened to us once, with very thoroughly cut-up and firmly compressed lemon peels. The next time you use the still, only fill it about three-fourths of the way full, boil it at a lower heat, and consider adding a couple of drops of antifoam (spread a small dash of it directly over the chopped-up plants in the already-filled kettle). Antifoam, an aqueous emulsion of polydimethylsiloxane (PDMS, also known as dimethicone, a certain kind of silicone oil, nontoxic and chemically inert), prevents foam from forming. This emulsion is added to alcoholic mashes before the distillation, so it's usually available at specialty winemaking and distilling stores.

Don't switch out the distillate bottle until it's full. If you're working with 1.5 quarts (1.5 liters) of water, you can fill up to five 6.8-ounce (200-milliliter) bottles but no more without risking the still running dry. You should always be able to hear the sound of boiling. If you hear hissing instead, there's no water left in the kettle. If this happens, you should immediately remove the still from the heat.

With most plants, you'll notice that the majority of the oil collects in the first bottle. It's only with very hard and tough products that most of it will be in the second. The amount per bottle then decreases sharply, to the extent that it's pointless to fill more than three or four bottles.

Why not just collect all of the distillate in one large bottle? There are two reasons. First of all, most of the oil appears at the beginning, and you're eventually distilling almost pure water, so some of the oil would end up dissolving in the additional water. Second, different qualities of oil appear depending on how long

Note: The distilling conditions (how long you distill, the pressure and temperature of the steam, the design of the still) can have a significant effect on the amount, composition, and quality of the essential oils.

you've been distilling. The earlier the oil comes out, the less time it spent exposed to high temperatures, making its quality correspondingly better. In a big bottle, oils with these varying levels of quality would all mix together. A good example is the differing qualities of ylang-ylang oil (see page 92) that you get from large stills when you switch out the receiver container during distillation, the so-called fractional distillation or fractioning as previously mentioned.

> ☺ Tip: Some wood, bark, roots, and hard seeds don't give up their essential oils easily. In these cases, it's a good idea to use very salty water (table salt) in the distillation and/or soak the chopped-up material in it for a few weeks beforehand.

When distilling resin: Put the resin in the freezer. When frozen, smash it with a big hammer into tiny pieces. Mix the pieces with beechwood chips, which are available in hardware stores, pour at a ratio of 1:1. Fill the mixture in the still and distill as usual. The still won't get clogged because the resin will stick to the chips. The small amount of resin residue stuck to the still walls can be removed with acetone. By the way, it's worth distilling resins; their yield is about 30–40 percent.

Double distillation

Rose oil distillation makes use of a somewhat different process. Due to its low oil content, the rose petals are double distilled.

First distillation

Distill the fresh rose petals as described earlier. The distillate will only include a very small oil layer called the *raw rose oil* or the first rose fraction. The hydrosol is the *oil water*. The amount of oil produced can vary depending on the type of rose and how mature it was. If there's enough to separate it from the hydrosol, remove the oil layer (see separating the hydrosol and the oil, page 48) and continue to work with the oil water. If there's not enough oil to separate it, shake the hydrosol vigorously before using it any further.

Second distillation

Place the hydrosol from the first distillation into the freshly cleaned still and distill it. Another thin oil film will form on the new distillate. The hydrosol is the famous rosewater; the oil is the second rose fraction. The second distillation is also known as *cohobation*.

Now you can combine the first and second rose fractions—this mixture produces the classic rose oil. Industrially produced rose oils, such as those from Isparta (Turkey), consist of about 35 percent from the first fraction and 65 percent from the second fraction.

The same process used for rose oil (i.e., distilling the hydrosol a second time) also works with any other type of plant. It's especially useful for achieving good results with plants that produce less oil.

Another option is to also add additional fresh plant material to the steamer basket during the second distillation. As a rule, you

Note: Using a hydrosol instead of fresh water increases your oil yield.

should never distill less than 1.5 quarts (1.5 liters) of hydrosol each time or else an oil layer won't form because there's not enough oil. This is still true even if you also add fresh material.

Separating the hydrosol and the oil

▲ Jerkily rotate the bottles in both directions about their long axes multiple times to release the oil drops from the glass wall.

The oil immediately separates from the water as soon as the liquid leaves the condenser. With very small quantities, the distillate is just cloudy, without a floating oil layer.

You should store the distillate in sealed bottles for at least two to four weeks in a cool, dark location before separating the oil. During this time, the hydrosol and the oil layer are able to optimally separate from each other. If this doesn't happen despite storing it for a long time, you can also try to induce the separation by adding salt (at least about 1.5–3.8 ounces per quart [50–100 grams per liter] of sodium chloride, sodium sulfate, magnesium sulfate, ammonium chloride, etc.). The salt increases the surface tension of the watery layer, causing it to separate from the oil better. If you quickly, jerkily spin the bottles back and forth around their long axis while they're in storage, the drops of oil stuck to the sides will also climb upward or sink downward, but make sure not to shake the bottles vertically. There are several different ways to separate the oil.

Oils lighter than water

Syringe

In our opinion, the best and easiest method is to remove the oil with syringes and thick hypodermic needles. Depending on how much oil there is, 2- to 10-milliliter syringes of the type available in pharmacies and medical supply stores will work. Even the smallest amounts of oil can be sucked out very effectively in this manner. Be aware that in the United States laws on buying syringes and needles over the counter vary from state to state.

Hold the bottle in one hand and the syringe with the attached needle in the other. Insert the needle until it is just above the surface of the water (i.e., on the bottom edge of the oil layer). Then slowly fill the syringe using your thumb and index finger. If you suck up any water, just knock your finger against the syringe and spurt the water back in the bottle.

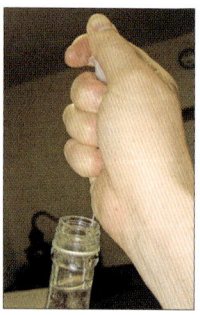

▲ Insert the syringe until it's just above the hydrosol and fill.

Now read off the exact amount of oil you collected in the syringe. This is important for calculating the yield. Note down the volume and pour the oil into small, dark oil bottles (see storing the oil). Repeat this process with the other bottles of distillate until you've extracted all of the oil. If you want to keep the fractions separate, put the oil from each distillate container into a different oil bottle.

Making Your Own Oil, Step by Step

◀ Some oils, such as cinnamon oil, are heavier than water.

Oils heavier than water

It's best to use a container that comes to a narrow point at the bottom. With prosecco or piccolo champagne bottles, for example, you have the advantage of the bottom not being flat, but rather protruding upward in the middle. This means that there's a deep groove around the edge for the oil to collect in. Unfortunately, a regular needle is too short to extract the oil from there. You can use a glass Pasteur pipette and a short piece of silicone hose instead. The silicone tube serves as a connecter between the syringe and the pipette. You can then suck up the oil as usual and read off the volume: the value right where the syringe's plunger is is the amount of oil. Only collect oil in the pipette, not in the silicone hose, which is difficult to clean.

Pipette

Pipettes also do a good job of extracting the essential oil, as long as you use glass pipettes with a long, thin end. Normal pipettes, like the ones in a medical kit, won't work well. They're too short and usually have an end that's much too thick. Graduated pipettes aren't thin enough either.

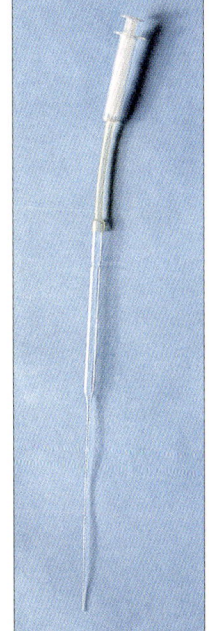

▲ Use a syringe with silicone hose and Pasteur pipette for sucking up heavier oils.

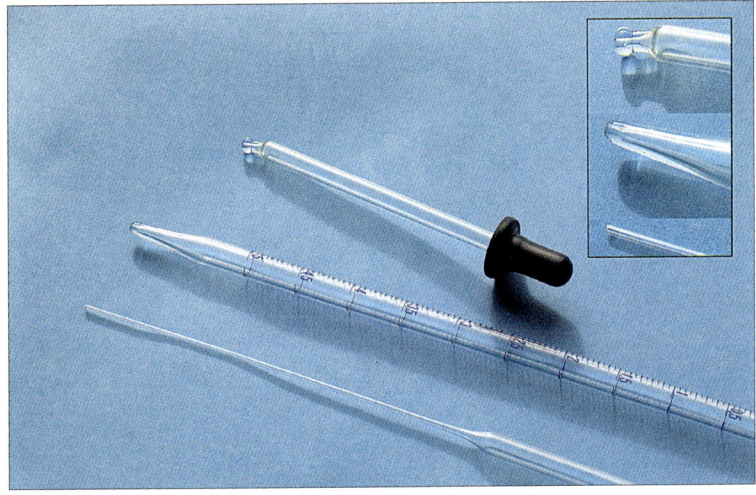

◀ Pasteur pipette, graduated pipette, and medical pipette with their points (detailed view top right)

The process is similar to using a syringe. Insert the thin glass capillary tube until it reaches the bottom of the oil layer and suck up the oil. The differences from when you use a syringe are that you can't read off the oil volume and that if you accidentally suck up some of the water, you can't get rid of it without losing some of the oil too.

Separatory funnel

Oils lighter than water

The so-called separatory funnel is the classic device for separating oil from water, or any two immiscible liquids from each other, in a laboratory setting. It has the form of a glass balloon that gets narrower and narrower toward the bottom. At the bottom is an outlet valve, and at the top is a nozzle for filling.

Pour the water-oil mixture into the top of the funnel, close the nozzle and shake, then leave it standing still for about twenty minutes so that the two layers can fully separate from each other. Essential oils usually float on the top, with the watery layer, the hydrosol, underneath. Next, open the valve at the bottom end of the funnel so that the hydrosol can flow out. As soon as the oil layer reaches the outlet valve, close it so that only the complete oil layer remains in the funnel. It can then be emptied into another container.

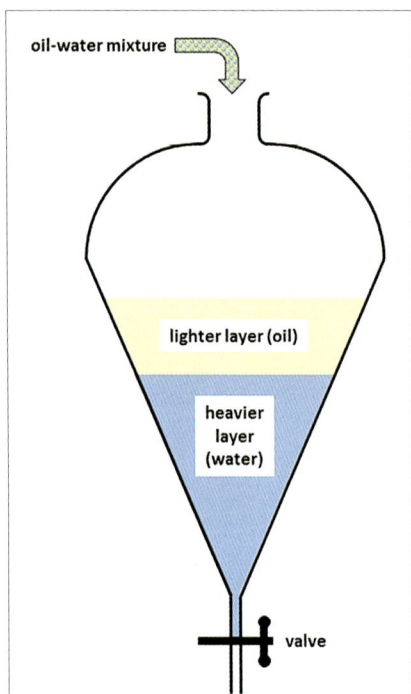

▲ Separatory funnel

It's very simple to separate two immiscible liquids with a separatory funnel. However, this method only works with essential oils to a limited extent. There's usually a very low amount of oil such that when the oil layer moves further and further downward as the watery layer is drained out, it eventually all ends up attached to the glass surface. This can happen so completely that no oil can be drained out at all at the end because it's all spread over the glass. Consequently, a separatory funnel only makes sense for larger oil volumes.

However, the separatory funnel has the same problem as the pipette: you can't determine the volume of the oil precisely enough. It's nevertheless very useful for shaking out the hydrosol (see chapter 5 and the introduction).

Oils heavier than water

This method works great with essential oils that are heavier than water. The oil will collect at the narrow bottom part of the funnel on its own from the beginning and will be the first thing that comes out.

Automatic oil separator

Oil stills are often offered with an automatic oil separator. The distillate is collected in a sort of glass pipe, and a tube connected to the lower third of this pipe automatically carries the hydrosol back into the kettle. This design isn't a very good choice for producing essential oils (not useful at all to receive hydrosols), especially if you hope to create a high-quality product, for the following reasons:

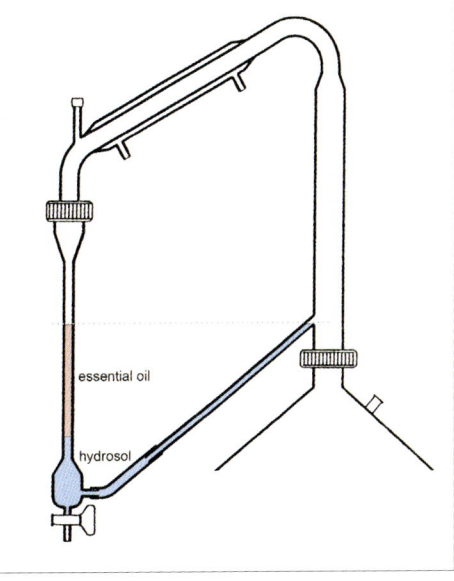

- The automatic recirculation doesn't give the oil any time to sit still and separate from the water, so some of the oil is always carried along into the kettle.
- If you distill an oil that's heavier than water, the oil will be carried back into the kettle instead of the watery layer. This makes the whole still useless.
- The recirculation into the kettle causes the hydrosol and part of the essential oil to be repeatedly reheated. Part of the aromatic substances will be overcooked and the oil will take on a lightly burned smell.
- Fine fractioning is impossible. The especially high-quality fractions that normally come out of the still first are always mixed together with the parts that boil for a longer time. Of course it's possible to empty the collecting pipe more frequently, but then you'll lose much of the recirculating hydrosol (i.e., the volume of the recycling system will become smaller and smaller).

▲ Automatic oil separator: the hydrosol-oil mixture flows in the left tube, where the oil separates from the hydrosol. The oil is the lighter phase, so it remains at the top and cannot reach the bottom. The hydrosol (lower phase) is led back to the still head via a connection tube.

Why are stills like this even sold if they have such serious drawbacks? Their big benefit is that you need very little water to carry out distillation with recirculation. The oil-saturated water is carried back into the still, increasing your yield. However, you can replicate this one positive trait by using your hydrosol in place of fresh water the next time you distill. You'll still see an increased yield, but not at the expense of quality, which should be your first priority when you make your own oil.

Recirculating the hydrosol, by the way, is why ylang-ylang/cananga oil is offered at several different quality grades. The highest grades of oil are separated at the beginning, the lowest after several days of recirculating distillation.

▲ Essencier (Florentine flask) in rose oil distillation

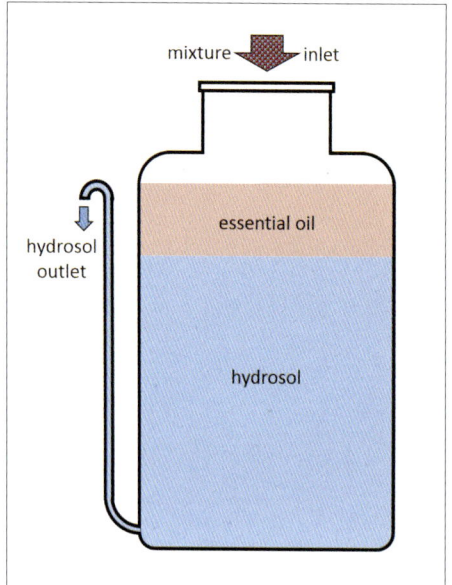 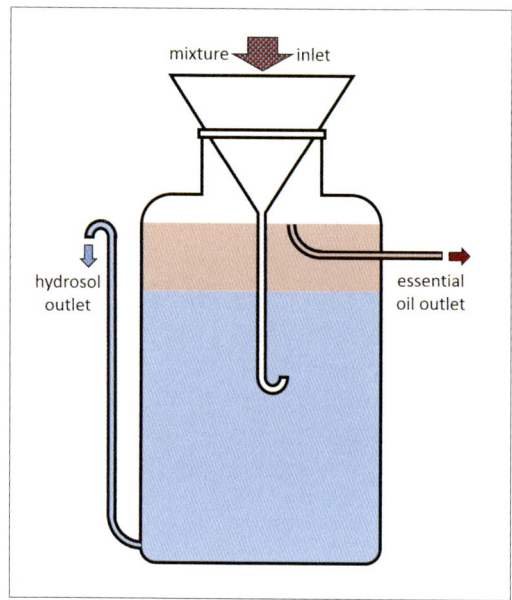

▲ Florentine flask or essencier (left), variant with oil outlet (right).

Florentine flask or essencier

In industrial production, the oil separation is usually carried out using a Florentine flask or essencier. Depending on the amount of oil, there are two different types: in the classic design only the hydrosol drains out, whereas with the larger version the essential oil also continually drains out too. As you can see in the accompanying picture, the classic essencier looks like a watering can: the oil-hydrosol mixture enters the container and the light oil collects at the top while the hydrosol flows out through the spout. In the larger version, the essential oil also flows out through an overflow pipe. Since the container is large in both cases, the distillate spends a lot of time just sitting, allowing the oil to separate thoroughly from the watery layer.

Cleanliness

Note: Clean syringes, pipettes, etc., with alcohol after every time you use them.

During the oil separation stage, you should be particularly careful to make sure that the equipment you use (syringes and bottles) is clean. Get in the habit of washing syringes with clean, non-denatured alcohol (at least 80 percent ABV) after every time you use them. Fill the syringe with alcohol and then empty it into another container; otherwise the alcohol will become increasingly impure.

Always keep other equipment such as pipettes, glass bottles, etc., very clean as well. This will ensure that no oils mix together due to unclean conditions.

Making Your Own Oil, Step by Step

Calculating the yield

Once you've separated out all the oil from the steam distillation, you can calculate the percent of your yield, enabling you to compare different charges of a particular plant or different plant varieties. A rule of thumb for dried herbs and seeds is the higher the yield, the better the quality of the material used. Old or inappropriately dried material has a significantly lower yield.*

$$\frac{\text{Oil volume (milliliters)}}{\text{Plant mass (grams)}} \times 100 = \text{yield in percent}$$

◀ Example

Plant mass: 656 grams of dried bay leaves, chopped up
Oil collected: Bottle 1: 5.0 milliliters
Bottle 2: 2.0 milliliters
Bottle 3: 1.0 milliliters
Bottle 4: 0.2 milliliters
Total: 8.2 milliliters

8.2 / 656 · 100 = 1.25 percent

Yield from:
▶ Orange peels
(whole peels, distilled instead of pressed):
Bottle I: 5.6 milliliters
Bottle II: 3.4 milliliters
Bottle III: 0.8 milliliters
Total: 9.8 milliliters

Initial weight was:
4.39 pounds (1,991 grams)
hence:
approximate yield: 9.8 / 1,991 · 100
= 0.49 percent
along with about 16.9 U.S. fluid ounces (500 milliliters) of orange hydrosol (orange water)

Yield from:
▶ Rose balm
(leaves and blossoms, fresh):
Bottle I: 4.6 milliliters
Bottle II: 1.1 milliliters
Bottle III: 1.0 milliliters
Total: 6.7 milliliters

Initial weight was:
1.33 pounds (604 grams)
hence:
approximate yield: 6.7 / 604 · 100
= 1.1 percent
along with about 16.9 U.S. fluid ounces (500 milliliters) of rose balm hydrosol

Yield from:
▶ Lemon peels
(whole peels, distilled instead of pressed):
Bottle I: 6.4 milliliters
Bottle II: 0.8 milliliters
Bottle III: 0.4 milliliters
Total: 7.6 milliliters

Initial weight was:
3.73 pounds (1,692 grams)
hence:
approximate yield: 7.6 / 1692 · 100
= 0.45 percent
along with about 16.9 U.S. fluid ounces (500 milliliters) of lemon hydrosol

---

* All non-metric units given in U.S. standard customary units.

For the sake of completeness, we should mention that the density of the oil normally has to be taken into account. If the upper equation is written again with units, it makes clear why this is actually like comparing apples and oranges: 8.2 milliliters / 656 grams · 100 = 1.25 … which unit? The unit percent cannot be "volume divided by weight." Both values of the division must have the same unit. With metric units, this calculation is good enough for our purposes, however. Because by definition 1 milliliter of water is 1 gram (density is 1 gram per milliliter), in the case of water, milliliters is the same as grams. Most essential oils have a density between 0.8 and 1.1 grams per milliliter. Thus, the deviation of this approach is approximately between +20 and -10 percent of the true value.

Depending on the plant variety, the typical oil yield is between 0.05 to 50 milliliters per 3.7 quarts (3.5 liters) of cut-up plant material (i.e., about 0.9–2.2 pounds or 0.4–1 kilograms), with an average of up to 20 milliliters. Since the essential oil is so highly concentrated, you can still produce useful amounts even from this "low" yield. Just 1 milliliter of essential oil is enough for 5 milliliters of perfume, 7 pounds (3.3 kilograms) of soap, 1 quart (1 liter) of massage oil, or 27 fluid ounces (800 milliliters) of facial oil.

Cold pressing

Materials list
- 5 lemons (or other citrus fruit)
- Small grater
- Metal tea strainer
- Teaspoon
- 1 small cup

Cost: about U.S.$7 (€5)

The cold pressing process is often used to produce base oils such as corn oil, olive oil, almond oil, etc. For our purposes, it is useful for citrus fruits such as oranges, lemons, tangerines, bergamots, grapefruits, etc.

Since most households don't contain a special press for this process, we'll approach this method a little differently.

It's best to use natural, untreated lemons, of course, because their peels don't have an artificial wax layer. Otherwise, clean the peel thoroughly with dish soap and a brush. Zest the lemon with a grater. Take the zest and place it in a tea strainer. Use a teaspoon to squeeze the zest over a cup so that a mixture of lemon oil and an aqueous liquid drips into it. Depending on what you're doing with it next, you can either use this mixture directly or let it sit for a few days until the oil separates from the aqueous phase and the cloudy material. Then you can separate the oil with a syringe (see page 48) and mix it with 96 percent ABV alcohol (at least 80 percent) to make a perfume base, for example (see page 110).

Making Your Own Oil, Step by Step

Cold pressing

◂ You need the following materials for cold pressing: lemons, a small grater, a metal tea strainer, a teaspoon, and a small cup

Zest the untreated lemons into the sieve above the cup ▸

◂ Put the entire ground mass in the strainer

and press it out with the teaspoon ▶

◀ Your result will be a mixture of lemon oil and a kind of hydrosol.

Maceration

This method of production relies on the ability of fatty oils to extract the fragrance from blossoms and herbs. Any of the plants listed in the note on enfleurage and solvent extraction in chapter 4 can also undergo maceration. You should only use the finest odorless fatty oils. In addition to the carrier oils listed in chapter 5, almond or peach kernel oil, ben oil, or the best varieties of olive oil work well. It's best to place the blossoms in a tea strainer or a teaball that is as large as possible and then to submerge the whole thing in the fatty oil. After a few days, once the blossoms have lost their scent, remove them, press them out, and add new fresh ones. The optimal infusion time differs from plant to plant, but it's generally somewhere between one day and one week. You shouldn't leave the blossoms in the oil for too long or it will take on an herbaceous smell.

Now that the oil has been enriched with the blossoms' fragrance, you can either use it directly in your products or treat it with rectified spirit (96 percent ABV, at least 80 percent) as described in the next section.

Enfleurage

Enfleurage is an especially good method for subtle flower fragrances like jasmine, rose, or violet. Fat is used to extract the oil instead of a chemical solvent, so the oil can be unhesitatingly used in your products afterward. Lard or tallow are the classic enfleurage fats, but you can also use other fats such as coconut oil, palm butter, shea butter, Vaseline, or a mixture of Vaseline (70 percent) and glycerin (30 percent), for example. If you want to make the fat directly into a cream or something similar after enfleurage, it's a good idea to use plant fats for their healthful ingredients.

> ☺ Tip: If you use lard as the enfleurage fat, you should purify it first as follows: First, melt it at a very low heat and then boil it in a solution of about 15 grams per liter of alum (aluminum potassium sulfate) and about 15 grams per liter of table salt in diluted sodium hydroxide solution (2.0 grams per liter).

Spread 1–2 centimeters of fat onto a glass plate. Place the petals on the fat, press them lightly, and cover with a second glass plate. Place a wooden frame on the lower plate before you cover it; the upper plate shouldn't touch the fat or the blossoms. Remove the blossoms after one to two days, ideally with tweezers, and add new blossoms. Repeat this process for one to two months, at which point the fat will be heavily saturated with the essential oil. Use the fat quickly because its smell can turn rancid relatively easily; store the fat with the extracting blossoms at a cool place (such as a cellar) during the entire process for the same reason.

Then use a wooden spatula to move the fat into a glass container and fill it with alcohol. The volume of the alcohol should be approximately twice that of the fat. Stir it all together vigorously and seal the container airtight so that the alcohol and the oil don't evaporate. Stir the mixture once per day for the next two to three weeks.

Finally, pour the alcohol through a coffee filter. The result will be a clear alcoholic liquid that can be made directly into a perfume, for example. The fat, which will still be very fragrant, can be blended into a soap or cream, among other things.

Materials list
- A handful of petals (every 1–2 days)
- 2 glass plates
- About 3.5 ounces (100 grams) of lard (available for cooking in any supermarket), shea butter, cocoa butter, or vaseline
- About 7 ounces (200 milliliters) of 80–96 percent ABV pure alcohol
- Glass container (Erlenmeyer flask, canning jar, jam jar, etc.)
- Wooden spatula
- Tweezers
- Coffee filter

Cost: about U.S.$7 (€5)

The Essential Oil Maker's Handbook

You need the following materials for enfleurage: alcohol (greater than 80 percent ABV), a coffee filter, a measuring cup, tweezers, a wooden spatula, fat, a glass container, and two glass plates. ▶

Coat a glass plate with 0.4–0.8 inches (1–2 centimeters) of fat. ▶

Place the petals onto the fat and push them gently. ▶

Making Your Own Oil, Step by Step

◂ Replace the petals with fresh ones after one or two days, ideally with tweezers. Repeat this for several weeks.

◂ Scrape the oil-saturated fat off of the glass plate and pour it into the glass container.

◂ Fill it with alcohol.

The Essential Oil Maker's Handbook

▲ Stir the mixture vigorously and seal the container airtight for two to three weeks.

Then pour the alcohol through a coffee filter, giving you a clear alcoholic liquid. ▶

Storing oils

Essential oils should always be stored in dark, firmly sealed, glass bottles. You can get these in different sizes, from 1 milliliter to 17 fluid ounces (500 milliliters). It's best to store them in a dark room at a temperature below 68°F (20°C). Always store your oils in their pure forms so that you can combine them into different mixtures whenever you feel like it.

Don't forget to label every bottle with the type of oil, quantity (and perhaps yield), and date made. You'll notice that the fragrance doesn't fully develop until after a few weeks or months. Some oils, such as bay leaf oil or rose oil, on the other hand, are so intense in their pure forms that smelling them is hardly bearable. They don't exhibit their proper bouquet until they're diluted.

Excessively high and low temperatures

Citrus oils keep for the shortest length of time, so they should be stored under cool conditions and used within a year. Some essential oils such as anise, fennel, rose, or cedarwood naturally solidify at temperatures below 46.4°F (8°C). They'll turn back to liquid form at room temperature (68°F or 20°C). Citrus oils and rose oil start to become cloudy at this temperature because they contain natural wax. You can filter it out, of course, but keep in mind that doing so also filters some of the oil's active ingredients. Thyme oil can crystallize at lower temperatures. If you put it in a 104°F (40°C) water bath, it will turn back into a liquid.

Many essential oils are easily flammable and should therefore always be stored in a secure location.

◀ Dark bottles for storing essential oils

The same rules for storing oils apply to storing hydrosols. You can mix them with alcohol into a 16 percent ABV solution to make them last longer. To reach this concentration, you'll need 8 fluid ounces of 80 percent ABV alcohol per quart hydrosol (250 milliliters of 80 percent ABV alcohol per liter hydrosol) or 6.4 fluid ounces per quart (200 milliliters per liter) of 96 percent ABV alcohol.

CHAPTER 4

Distillable Materials

This chapter will give you an overview of the most important raw materials that can be used to produce essential oils. We will cover both domestic and exotic plants, because why not distill some oil from the eucalyptus tree you're growing in your room the next time it gets too big and has to be pruned? We've also provided the scientific names of each plant species so that you can use a reference book to find the right varieties of plants unfamiliar to you.

All the information and descriptions given refer to steam distillation. Special cases are noted in their descriptions, and other production methods are also referenced. You can find an overview of the proper harvest times in the harvest calendar (page 134).

The given yields also refer to steam distillation. Please note, however, that the actual yield is heavily dependent on the plants' ripeness and exposure to sunlight. You should therefore think of these values as general benchmarks. It's generally sensible to work with at least about 3 quarts (3 liters) of finely chopped raw materials. This amount corresponds to, depending on the apparent density after (not too strong) tamping, approximately 1.1–2.2 pounds (0.5–1 kilogram). The table below gives you a few examples of yields.

We intentionally only briefly discuss the effects of the various oils because we don't have room here to give that subject the treatment it deserves and wish to concentrate solely on production.

Material	Amount		Yield [ml]
	[oz.]	[g]	
Anise seeds	35	1,000	12.3
Bay leaves, dried	21	600	8.7
Bee balm, fresh	21	600	6.7
Caraway seeds	35	1,000	10.3
Cinnamon sticks, chopped	28	790	9.1
Cloves, dried	21	600	10.4
Eucalyptus, fresh	28	800	5.5
Fennel, fresh	35	1,000	5.4
Juniper berries, dried	35	1,000	9.8
Lavender blossoms, dried	14	400	12.0

◀ Examples of yields from the Leonardo Classic still

Lemon peels (whole peels)	60	1,690	7.6
Mint, green, dried	18	500	5.8
Mint, Japanese, fresh	28	800	8.2
Orange peels (whole peels)	70	1,990	9.8
Oregano, dried	14	400	5.7
Peppermint, fresh	27	760	8.4
Rosemary, dried	25	700	8.5

Types of plants

Allspice/ pimento *(Pimenta officinalis)*

First crush the unripe, dried fruits with a mortar and pestle and then distill them. The oil smells similar to clove oil and is also heavier than water (see clove).
Effects: antiseptic, settles the stomach, appetite stimulant, alleviates rheumatism and muscle pain
Yield: 3–4 percent

Angelica *(Angelica archangelica)*

Angelica is an old healing plant from the north that is as tall as a person. It used to found in every garden but is now more commonly found in overgrown areas.

The root or the full rhizome is usually used in oil distillation. The oil from the seeds doesn't smell as nice. Before distilling, cut up the root very thoroughly; crush it if possible. In commercial production, the roots are cut into small pieces and then stored for two to three years. They are harvested in the fall of the second or third year after blooming. Don't handle angelica before spending time in the sun as it leaves stains on your skin.
Warning: Despite its size, angelica is sometimes confused with the deadly cowbane. You should be sure that you're very familiar with the plant before collecting it.
Effects: antibacterial, dissolves mucus, relieves pain, calming, improves circulation
Yield: root: 0.3–1 percent, seeds: 0.8–1.1 percent

▲ Anise seeds

Anise, star anise *(Pimpinella anisum, Illicium verum)*

The essential oil is located in the seeds. To get as much as possible, lightly crush the anise seeds with a mortar and pestle before distilling. You can find the seeds in the spice aisle of any supermarket under the label of "Anise Seed Whole." Make sure not to pack the seeds into the still too densely or an excess in pressure may form.

You should only use anise oil externally. Keep the parts of your skin that you use it on out of direct sunlight.
Effects: calming, aids sleep, alleviates coughing and colds, strengthens the stomach, relieves cramps
Yield: anise seed: 2–3.5 percent, star anise: 1–5 percent

Balm, lemon balm, bee balm
(Melissa officinalis, Monarda didyma, Monarda fistulosa)

The classic lemon balm (*Melissa officinalis*), also known simply as balm, is currently a subject of significant interest among many researchers: when should it be harvested to maximize your oil yield? Results have ranged from in the morning before sunrise to the peak of the midday sun. We've achieved our best results by harvesting them early in the afternoon, when it's hottest out. In our view, the only important thing is for the days prior to the harvest to have been sunny. Harvest the full plants from June through September late in their bloom, and distill them immediately afterward. Their oil output is low, so you'll need about 7.7 tons (7,000 kilograms) of lemon balm to produce 1 quart (1 liter) of oil, making double distillation a good idea in this case as well. Melissa oil is currently among the most expensive in the world: 1 quart (1 liter) of it can cost upward of U.S.$6,000.

Bee balm (*Monarda didyma, M. fistulosa*) is a representative of another plant genus, Monarda, which is often also wrongly called balm. *M. didyma* is a beautiful plant with red blossoms and *M. fistulosa* has purple blossoms, an intense aroma, and produces much more oil than lemon balm. With bee balm, you should also use the whole plant while it's in bloom.

Effects: lemon balm: relieves cramps, calming, reduces headaches, balances and exhilarates, moderates digestive and heart issues. Bee balm: stimulant, dissolves mucus, induces sweating, diuretic, helps wounds heal, regulates the menstrual cycle, anthelmintic, settles the stomach, alleviates headaches, fevers, and bronchitis

Yield: lemon balm: 0.015–0.1 percent; bee balm: 0.5–1 percent

▲ Distillation of 14 ounces (400 grams) of dried lavender blossoms with the Leonardo Classic still

Balsam poplar
(Populus balsamifera L.)

This American poplar has resinous leaves that smell strongly like pine needles. Its balsamic fragrance exudes even more strongly from the resin from its buds and young shoots. Usually extract

◀ Top left: Branches and wood of the balsam poplar, without leaves or buds. Bottom: Chopped-up pieces of the branches and wood. Top right: Balsam poplar oil (heavier than water) and hydrosol from the chopped-up wood.

The Essential Oil Maker's Handbook

▲ Lemon basil

from the buds is used to make shampoos, but you can also extract the essential oil from the buds, leaves, twigs, and wood in the usual way via steam distillation. Since balsam poplar oil is heavier than water, it collects at the bottom of the receiver container. Native Americans used the resin against colds, rheumatism, and burns.

Effects: actively supports hair structure, anti-inflammatory, disinfectant

Yield: buds: 30–40 percent resin; wood: 0.05–0.1 percent oil; leaves, shoots: 0.3–0.5 percent oil

Basil *(Ocimum basilicum)*

Cut up the entire herb. The oil can only be produced from the leaves and the blooming flower heads, however. Various different types of basil are available in stores. Other types such as lemon basil are also great for distilling. Don't use products made from basil oil on your face.

Effects: appetite stimulant, digestive, calming, relaxant, alleviates pain from stomach or menstrual issues, balm for the spirit and soul, antibacterial

Yield: 0.02–0.04 percent

Bay laurel *(Laurus nobilis)*

Cut up the fruits, leaves, and twigs. You can distill either fresh or dried plants.

Effects: antiseptic, digestive, strengthens the stomach, helps with dandruff and hair loss, stimulant, exhilarating

Yield: berries: 0.6–0.8 percent; leaves: fresh: 1.0–2.5 percent; dried: 0.8–1.5 percent

Bay rum tree/ West Indian bay tree *(Pimenta acris, P. racemosa)*

The bay oil is extracted by distilling the (cut-up) leaves, berry-like fruits, and young twig tips. The oil content is highest in June and July. The tree is principally native to the Caribbean island of Dominica (in the West Indies), where this oil is also made. There are three different types of fragrance: normal, anise, and citronella.

Effects: regenerating, cooling, supports tired and stressed skin

Yield: 2.3–2.6 percent (leaves)

Benzoin *(Styrax benzoin)*

The Sumatra benzoin tree grows up to 66 feet (20 meters) tall and has leaves that are up to 4 inches (10 centimeters) wide and inflorescences (flower clusters) that are up to 7 inches (18 centimeters) long with white blossoms. Commercially, the oil is first extracted from the trees through solvent extraction and then via steam distillation. The resinoid process is common as well. The oil is often used as a fixative in perfume production and is a component of

incense. At a smaller scale, chopped-up branches can also be distilled, but they produce much less oil.
Effects: dissolves mucus, relieves cramps, alleviates tension and irritability as well as respiratory ailments
Yield: 20–40 percent

The peels of the small green fruits of the bergamot tree, a cross between bitter orange and lemon, can either be pressed or cut up and distilled (see lemon). Don't apply the oil to your skin before going sunbathing.
Effects: ameliorates unclean and oily skin, antidepressant, lowers fevers, appetite stimulant, improves mood, relaxant, alleviates fear and depression
Yield: 0.3–0.6 percent

Bergamot *(Citrus aurantium)*

Birch oil can be extracted from the leafy branches, the buds, or the soft outer bark of the tree, but only the bark is used for commercially produced sweet birch oil (*B. lenta*). Collect the bark or twigs and buds in May and June, cut them up, and distill them.
Effects: diuretic, detoxifying, helps prevent bladder stones and urinary tract infections, helps hair growth
Yield: 0.05–1 percent

Birch *(Betula lenta, B. alba)*

Neroli oil is produced by distilling fresh blossoms of the bitter orange tree. Along with jasmine and rose, it is one of the most expensive oils. The hydrosol from distilling is orange flower water.
Effects: antidepressant, calming, soporific, stimulates the growth of skin cells
Yield: 0.07–0.1 percent

Bitter orange/ neroli *(Citrus aurantium)*

Like neroli oil, this beloved oil comes from the bitter orange tree, but in this case you use its leaves, twigs, and buds along with unripe fruits. You can also make petitgrain oil from the leaves of lemon and tangerine trees.
Effects: calming, improves concentration, antidepressant, alleviates respiratory issues
Yield: 0.2–0.4 percent

Bitter orange/ petitgrain *(Citrus aurantium, C. limonum, C. reticulata, C. amara, C. bigaradier)*

Oils obtained from the blossoms of the broom bush are made industrially via enfleurage or solvent extraction. Steam distillation is possible too, but you'll have to perform a double distillation due to the very small amount of oil produced. Put the hydrosol in the kettle for the second distillation and add more fresh blossoms. Only use the oil and hydrosol externally.
Effects: mood-lifting and invigorating, relaxant
Yield: 0.05–0.09 percent

Broom *(Spartium junceum)*

Cajuput
(Melaleuca leucadendron)

This plant belongs to the myrtle family and is native to Southeast Asia. Cut up and distill the fresh leaves and twigs of the cajuput tree.
Effects: germicidal, alleviates respiratory ailments and the flu along with skin problems, relaxant, improves circulation
Yield: 0.8–1 percent

Camphor
(Cinnamomum camphora)

The fresh wood of the camphor tree is used in steam distillation. Chop up the wood into 0.5-by-0.5-centimeter pieces. Only use the oil and hydrosol externally.
Effects: alleviates colds, antidepressant
Yield: 3–4 percent

Caraway
(Carum carvi),
Cumin
(Cuminum cyminum)

Use ripe caraway seeds (*Carum carvi*). Before distilling, gently crush them with a mortar and pestle. In our experience, caraway seeds, depending on where they originated, can swell up quickly in the steam. You should therefore only fill the still about three-quarters full to keep the kettle and the middle part from scattering apart during the distillation.

Cumin oil and hydrosol (*Cuminum cyminum*) have a refreshing anise-like smell in contrast to caraway, so don't confuse both varieties when using them as food additive.
Warning: Caraway and cumin oil can cause skin irritation, so test out a few drops on the crook of your arm before using it.
Effects: relieves cramps, appetite stimulant, improves digestion and metabolism
Yield: 3–7 percent

▲ Caraway oil and hydrosol

Cardamom
(Elettaria cardamomum)

Cardamom belongs to the ginger family. However, its seeds are distilled, not its roots.
Effects: improves circulation, relieves digestive issues, improves your mood
Yield: 4–7 percent

Caraway seeds (left) and cumin seeds (right) ▶

It's important to distinguish between the cedrus varieties (Atlas, Himalayan, and Cyprus cedars) and the North American juniper species, the eastern red cedar (*J. virginiana*). The effects listed below only apply to the cedrus varieties; the eastern red cedar is highly toxic, with a lethal dose of just six drops! Unfortunately, the species are often not differentiated in the literature, resulting in cedar oil and cedar leaf oil being warned against categorically because there have been many cases of poisoning already. True cedar oil is comparatively harmless, though, and is fine to use therapeutically.

Distill cedarwood that has been chopped up as thoroughly as possible. The leaves can also be distilled, but their oil has a different fragrance from oil extracted from the wood. Sadly, most cedar oils sold in stores are fake, originating from the eastern red cedar instead of the cedrus varieties. True cedar oil does not actually have an abortifacient effect, as is often warned about. Thuja oil is also often falsely sold as cedar leaf oil. Thuja oil is toxic due to its high thujone content, whereas cedar oil does not contain any thujone at all.

Effects: antiseptic, dissolves mucus, regenerating, gives strength and clarity, alleviates respiratory illnesses, relieves stress
Yield: 2.5–4.5 percent

Cedar
(Cedrus atlantica, C. brevifolia, C. deodara, Juniperus virginiana)

▲ Chamomile oil from German chamomile

The plant's seeds, leaves, and twigs are collected in September and distilled. Gently crush the seeds with a mortar and pestle. If you use the herb, prepare it with a kitchen shredder first. Oil extracted from the seeds doesn't smell as nice as oil from the leaves.
Effects: purifies the blood, alleviates throat and urinary diseases
Yield: herb: 0.05–0.1 percent; seeds: 2.5–3.0 percent

Celery
(Apium graveolens)

Only the blossoms are used in oil production. With Roman chamomile (*A. nobilis*), they're dried first, but German chamomile (*M. chamomilla*), they should be used fresh to maximize your oil yield. Only collect the blossoms of plants that have just recently bloomed. There are different varieties of chamomile, with *M. chamomilla* and *M. recutia* the most well-known. When you distill chamomile, you should put a paper towel or a cloth on the steamer basket so that the fine pieces of the blossoms don't fall to the bottom of the kettle and burn. If you use German chamomile, your result will be a beautiful dark blue oil, the color of which comes from its high azulene content formed by the steam (this blue oil is extremely valuable and expensive). We tried to distill oil from the dried chamomile available from the pharmacy once. We produced a negligible amount of oil; all we saw were a couple of blue streaks. With dried herbs, your success will always depend on whether the plants were harvested at the right time (after getting a lot of

Chamomile
(Matricaria chamomilla, M. recutia, M. discoidea, Anthemis nobilis, Chamaemelum nobile)

sunshine), whether they were dried properly, and the age of the dried material.
Effects: anti-inflammatory, alleviates allergic reactions as well as rheumatism and skin problems, relieves cramps, relaxant
Yield: German chamomile: 0.05–0.1 percent; Roman chamomile: 0.8–1.0 percent

Cilantro
(Coriandrum sativum)

Similarly to anise and fennel, it is the cilantro seeds that are used in making essential oil. They are harvested from the end of August through the beginning of September. As soon as the plant's seed heads change color, the herb can be cut and dried. Then gently shake the seeds and crush them thoroughly with a mortar and pestle before distilling. Cilantro oil makes a very good fixative for perfume production.
Effects: relieves cramps, alleviates stomach and bowel pains, relieves pain from rheumatism and joint pain
Yield: 0.1–0.8 percent

Cinnamon
(Cinnamomum zeylanicum, C. cassia)

You can extract the oil from dried cinnamon bark (*C. zeylanicum* and *C. cassia*) or from the branches, leaves, and blossoms (*C. zeylanicum*). Cinnamon bark is easier to acquire in regions where it is not cultivated. Chop up the bark thoroughly before distilling it: the best way is to wrap it in a cloth and hit it with a hammer. You will notice that cinnamon oil is one of the few oils that are heavier than water, which means that it collects at the bottom of the receiver container. As always, the quality of your raw plant material affects how much oil you extract. Once, for the sake of convenience, we bought cinnamon bark at a supermarket instead of from a spice dealer like we usually do. The price per kilogram was the same, but it only produced a third as much oil! You can look at distillation as a very effective quality control instrument for products that contain oil. Never use cinnamon oil internally.
Effects: bark: antiseptic, improves and stimulates circulation; leaves, etc.: very soothing to the skin, relaxant, relieves cramps
Yield: bark: 0.5–0.8 percent, leaves: 1–1.5 percent

Citronella

See lemongrass.

Clary sage
(Salvia sclarea)

Cut up and distill the ends of the herb. It's important to dry the plant first or your oil will smell disgusting.
Effects: calming, lowers blood pressure, relieves cramps, relaxant, alleviates respiratory diseases
Yield: 0.1–1 percent

◀ Clove oil is heavier than water. The two bottles contain a total of 8.5 milliliters of clove oil (from 1.3 pounds [600 grams] of dried cloves).

Clementine
(Citrus clementina)

Press the peels or cut them up and distill them (see lemon).
Effects: helps you fall asleep, improves wellness, warming
Yield: 0.5–0.7 percent

Clove
(Eugenia caryophyllata, Syzygium aromaticum)

Clove oil is usually extracted from the dried flower buds via steam distillation. Cutting or crushing the buds is unnecessary; they become thoroughly weak by the steam. Since the oil is heavier than water, it will collect at the *bottom* of the hydrosol bottle in the form of brown spheres. (Nearly) colorless oil is made via reflux distilling (see "fractional distillation"). Both the color and some of the active ingredients are lost during the second distillation. For clove stem oil, only the stems of the buds are used, but this type of oil doesn't have as fine of a fragrance as oil made from the buds. The leaves and roots can also be distilled. Oil made from the leaves doesn't irritate the skin as much as oil from the buds, while oil from the roots contains more of the irritating eugenol than the bud oil.

There are two easy ways to test the quality of cloves: if the dried flower buds feel greasy and secrete some oil when you press against the stem with a fingernail, they're of high quality and have a high oil content. Testing whether they float is also very enlightening: high-quality cloves sink in water or at least settle in a vertical position with the heads pointing upward because clove oil is heavier than water. Bad cloves that barely contain any more oil, on the other hand, float horizontally on the water's surface.

Warning: Don't apply pure clove oil directly to your skin because the ingredient eugenol irritates it.
Effects: stimulant, increases circulation, stimulates appetite and digestion, antiseptic, relieves cramps, excitatory, improves concentration
Yield: buds: 16–19 percent, roots: 4–5 percent

Cotton lavender
(Santolina chamaecyparissus)

Chop up and use the whole herb.
Effects: relieves cramps, helps the stomach, stimulant
Yield: 0.5–1 percent

Cypress
(Cupressus sempervirens)

You can cut up and use the twigs with their needles or use the fruits (cones) and blossoms.
Effects: balances hormones (during menopause), soothes hemorrhoids and varicose veins, nourishes the blood, calming, helps prevent cellulitis
Yield: 0.9–1.4 percent

Damiana
(Turnera diffusa)

This shrub is native to southwestern Texas, Central America, the Caribbean, and South America. Traditionally the leaves are used by the native people of Central America for tea and incense. Damiana has a stimulating effect on libido of both sexes, so it is used as an aphrodisiac, especially in Mexico where it's an accredited medication. The leaves are smoked, consumed as tea, or mixed in alcoholic beverages.

The steam-distilled essential oil and hydrosol have the same pleasant, sweetish-herbal scent as the (cut-up) dried leaves before distilling.
Effects: mental stimulant, relaxing, anxiolytic, aphrodisiac
Yield: dried leaves: 0.1–0.2 percent

Davana
(Artemisia pallens)

Distill the herb's yellow blossoms.
Effects: calming, mood-lifting and invigorating, relaxant, improves circulation
Yield: 0.05–0.5 percent

Dill
(Anethum graveolens)

You can use the whole herb, including the seeds. The oil is usually made exclusively from the seeds because they produce the most. Collect the seeds in the fall.
Effects: calming, digestive, appetite stimulant, dehydrating, relaxant
Yield: 2–4 percent (seeds)

Elecampane
(Inula helenium L.)

Elecampane is a large (about 6.6 feet or 2 meters) plant with yellow blossoms, somewhat similar to wolf's bane. It was once found in every cottage garden but is now only common in the mountains. The essential oil is found in the elecampane's rhizome; the oil is also known as helenin. It should be harvested between March and mid-April and between September and November (valid for European and North American continental climates).
Effects: dissolves mucus, alleviates coughing
Yield: 1–2 percent

Eucalyptus
(Eucalyptus globulus, E. radiata)

Eucalyptus trees can also grow in our part of the world just fine. The type matters, however: the "blue gum" eucalyptus contains the finest oil, but the tree doesn't do well in the winter. Cut up its leaves and twigs. The perfect harvest time is after the blossoms

Distillable Materials

◀ Large image: Eucalyptus (*E. globulus*) as a potted plant; only the uppermost left branch was used for distilling. Small image: 5.5 milliliters of eucalyptus oil made from 1.8 pounds (800 grams) of material.

have gone to seed. At our latitudes, however, blossoming unfortunately doesn't always take place.

Effects: lowers your blood sugar level, disinfectant, cooling, diuretic, improves respiration, stimulant, cheers you up, improves your concentration

Yield: fresh: 0.5–2 percent, dried: 3–4 percent

▲ Fennel seeds

The seeds are usually used for oil production—they can be either fresh or dried. They are harvested from the end of September through the beginning of October. Before distilling, gently crush the seeds with a mortar and pestle; this allows you to extract more oil. You can also distill the whole herb, but it provides a somewhat different scent.

Fennel
(Foeniculum vulgare, F. amara, F. dulce)

The Essential Oil Maker's Handbook

Effects: antitoxic, diuretic, inhibits cellulitis, strengthens the stomach, calming
Yield: 2–5 percent (seeds)

Fir, Douglas
(Abies alba, Pseudotsuga menziesii)

The particularly fine (white) fir oil can be extracted from chopped-up twig tips, needles, or cones. Mixing them is also possible. Collect the material between May and August; the essential oil is barely present in the winter because of the cold and lack of sun. One of the nicest needle fragrances comes from the Douglas fir, which also belongs to the pine family.
Effects: invigorating, soothes the airways, excitatory, warming
Yield: 0.7–1 percent

Frankincense
(Boswellia carterii, B. serrata)

The oil comes from the resin secreted by this small tree. Commercially, it's extracted via solvent extraction or the resinoid process. It should only be used externally.
Effects: deepens breathing, antidepressant, soothes the skin
Yield: solvent extraction: 5–9 percent; steam distillation: 0.4 percent

Garlic
(Allium sativum)

Distill chopped up garlic cloves. The scent is extremely intense. Harvest the garlic in August and September. Add a few drops of antifoam before starting the distillation.
Effects: antibacterial, lowers blood pressure and cholesterol, strengthens the heart
Yield: 0.1–0.4 percent

Geranium, storksbill, pelargonium
(Pelargonium graveolens, P. odoratissimum, P. capitatum, P. roseum, P. fragrans)

Do not confuse pelargoniums, commonly known as geraniums or storksbills, with true geraniums (also named cranesbills or hardy geraniums), the latter contain no oil and have no scent. You have the right plant if an intense scent is emitted when rubbing a leaf between your fingertips. Most scented pelargoniums have hairy leaves and small blossoms, whereas true geranium varieties with smooth leaves and large blossoms generally do not contain essential oils.

Use the leaves and the blooming flower heads. Most of the essential oil is contained in the young leaves. Don't cut the plant up too finely or it will turn into a pulp when you distill it. The plant must be blooming when you pick it. There are many different types of pelargoniums: Citriodorum, for example, smell like lemons. Rose-scented varieties produce oil similar to rose oil (30 percent of the ingredients are identical), but with a much higher yield. The so-called scented geranium oil produced via fractional distilling is often used as a substitute for rose oil for this reason.

▲ Scent "geranium"
(Pelargonium citriodorum)

Effects: lowers your blood sugar level, cleanses the liver and kidneys, relieves menopausal pains, stimulates very greasy or dry skin, calming, antiseptic, cleansing, invigorating, helps wounds heal, relieves anxiety, relieves dejection and discontent, antihemorrhagic
Yield: 0.1–1 percent

Ginger
(Zingiber officinale)

The roots can be distilled either fresh or dried. Dried roots produce an oil with a less spicy fragrance. It's true here too that the more you cut up the root, the more oil you'll get. We once tried to distill pure fresh ginger; the result was a foam bath and a big mess. So don't forget to add antifoam.
Effects: appetite stimulant, antiseptic, strengthens the stomach, alleviates motion sickness, improves circulation
Yield: 1.9–2.6 percent (dried)

Grapefruit
(Citrus grandis, C. paradisii)

See the lemon section; the same information applies to the grapefruit.
Effects: improves circulation, tightens and revitalizes the skin, inhibits cellulitis
Yield: 0.4–1 percent

Ground ivy
(Glechoma hederacea)

Ground ivy contains essential oil just like its relatives mint, thyme, and sage. Pick the plants while they're blooming in early summer.
Effects: alleviates colds and bronchitis, antihemorrhagic, tonic
Yield: 0.03–0.06 percent

Hemp
(Cannabis sativa)

Pick the young leaves and buds from the female plant between the end of September and the middle of October. Finely cut them up and distill them. Steam distillation does not extract the ingredient THC (tetrahydrocannabinol), so the resulting hemp oil does not have an intoxicating effect (intoxicating hemp oil is produced by solvent extraction). Don't use THC-free industrial hemp, which is especially cultivated for clothing materials and such. Its oil and hydrosol have a disgusting smell, whereas the distillate odor of a THC-variety is pleasantly strong, masculine, and warm, a bit like an autumn forest after the rain. It's therefore an excellent base note (see chapter 5) for men's fragrances.
Effects: appetite stimulant, calming, muscle relaxant, improves your mood, calms the skin, inhibits inflammation and nausea, painkilling, dilates the bronchial tubes, relieves intraocular pressure, repels gnats
Yield: 0.1–0.16 percent

Hogweed
(Heracleum sphondylium)

Hogweed is also described as "the ginseng of Europe." In Asia, it's sold as an aphrodisiac. The leaf stems and blossoms or the seeds are used for distillation. The green seeds have a strong lime scent.
Effects: digestion stimulant, lowers blood pressure, aphrodisiac
Yield: 0.1–0.5 percent

Hops
(Humulus lupulus)

Don't use the shoots; use the seed cones of the female plants. Harvest them in late summer. Make sure that the seed heads are still green or light yellow. Even wild hops are great for distilling.
Effects: antiseptic, appetite stimulant, digestive
Yield: 0.3–1 percent

Hyssop
(Hyssopus officinalis)

Cut up and distill the herb while it's in (late) bloom. Hyssop is generally used dried. Harvest it in the summer. Only use externally.
Effects: regulates circulation, helps with colds, calming
Yield: 0.3–0.9 percent

Iris
(Iris germanica var. florentina, I. pallida)

Making iris oil is relatively labor intensive. It takes three years for the plant to be ready to be harvested and for the roots to be ready to be dug out. Then you have to dry out and ferment the roots for three more years before you can peel, grind, and then distill them. The oil is extracted commercially through solvent extraction or via the resinoid process. It's usually solid like butter and colored yellow with a fine, very strong violet fragrance. It doesn't become a liquid until it's heated to about 104°F (40°C), but it already starts to congeal at 82°F (28°C). You should therefore make sure not to cool it too much during the distillation. Iris oil has a long shelf life, but you should store it dissolved in 96 percent ABV alcohol.
Effects: purifies the blood, harmonizing, helps the skin
Yield: 0.1–0.2 percent

Jasmine
(Jasminum officinale, J. grandiflorum)

Jasmine oil is produced commercially via solvent extraction. At home, however, it's better to make it using enfleurage. Pick the jasmine blossoms right after the buds sprout and the blossoms fully form. They must not be too old. Make sure that the enfleurage lasts at least three weeks—you'll have to cycle in fresh blossoms throughout this whole period. You should therefore begin working as soon as the shrub has its first blossoms. Pick them between July and October at sunrise, like roses. Jasmine blossoms give off their fragrance at night, so you can pick them after sunset too.
Effects: antidepressant, aphrodisiac, alleviates skin inflammation and headaches as well as uterine and menstrual issues, calming, improves your mood, relaxant
Yield: 0.07–0.1 percent

▲ Jasmine blossom

Distillable Materials

Juniper oil can be made either from fresh or completely or partially dried berries (altering the aroma somewhat). Crush the fruits before distilling them. You can also distill the twigs of the juniper tree. Commercially, the twigs are collected in the spring and the berries in the fall.
Effects: diuretic, appetite stimulant, cleanses the blood, alleviates stomach and intestinal issues, lowers blood sugar, invigorating, stimulant, disinfectant, inhibits cellulitis, relieves cramps
Yield: berries: 0.8–1.5 percent

Juniper
(Juniperus communis)

Use cut-up needles and twigs in the distillation. Like spruce, they should be collected between May and August.
Effects: alleviates asthma and other respiratory ailments
Yield: larch: 0.15–0.3 percent; larch resin: 14–15 percent

Larch
(Larix decidua)

Lavender oil is one of the most widespread varieties in the world. The oil can be extracted from the blossoms, panicles, stems, or leaves. It's also possible to distill the whole herb. The more haulm (stalk or stem) you use, however, the "woodier" your oil will be. Only the panicles (loosely branched flower clusters) or blossoms are used commercially. The plant is ready to be harvested as soon as the blossoms are withering on the panicle and the seeds are visible (around mid-August). It's the right moment when the bees or other insects no longer fly to the blossoms because of the lack of nectar. Harvest early in the afternoon in full sunlight to ensure the maximum possible oil content. Usually the fresh plants are tied into bundles and are hung upside down to let them dry for three days before distilling. However, we dry the panicles along with their long, thin stalks on a large sheet of packing paper as described in chapter 3. When dry, it's possible to shake off the blossoms from the stalks with ease.

Lavender and lavandin
(Lavandula officinalis, L. vera, L. angustifolia, L. spica, L. latifolia, L. stoechas; Lavandin grosso, Lavandin abrial)

Blooming lavandin ▼

▲ Wild growing juniper

There are many different varieties of lavender, such as classic lavender and spike lavender.

Lavandin has a special significance in oil production. It's a variety cultivated specifically for oil production in Provence, France. The plant contains a very high amount of oil. In contrast to regular lavender, however, it has no medicinal effects.

Effects: Lavender only: lowers blood pressure, alleviates skin ailments, calming, painkilling, invigorating, antiseptic, anti-inflammatory, hastens childbirth

Yield: lavender: herb: 0.5–1.5 percent; blossoms: 2.5–3 percent, lavandin: 3–5 percent

Lemon
(*Citrus medica, C. limonum*)

▲ Lemon

The classic method of oil production with lemons, as with all other citrus fruits, is cold pressing, but you can also achieve excellent results with steam distillation. In some parts of southern Europe the residue from the presses is distilled and mixed in with the pressed oil. It's rare to find pure, distilled citrus oils in stores, but when you do they will be labeled as citrus peel oils, such as, for example, lemon peel oil.

For the distillation, press the lemons with a citrus juicer and then cut up the leftover peels, first with scissors and then with a food processor or cutter mixer, and then distill them. You can increase your yield by peeling the fruits with a potato peeler and only cutting up and distilling the zest (see page 38).

With lemons, keep in mind that the amount of oil you produce depends on whether or not the fruit was picked when it was ripe. Try to use organic, untreated fruit because many lemons are treated with wax. If you're unable to find untreated fruit, scrub the peels thoroughly with dish soap and a brush. This should keep most impurities from making it into your oil.

Don't apply pressed citrus oil before sunbathing.

Effects: regulates circulation, alleviates arthritis and rheumatism as well as vein issues, stimulant, strengthening, improves circulation, stimulates metabolism, repels gnats

▲ Dried lemongrass

Yield: 0.03–1.4 percent

Lemon verbena
(*Lippia citriodora, Aloysia citriodora*)

Cut up and distill fresh or dried leaves and twigs.
Effects: relieves cramps, improves digestion and circulation
Yield: 0.1–0.3 percent

Lemongrass
(*Cymbopogon citratus, C. winterianus, C. nardus*)

You can distill fresh or dried blades of lemongrass. The plant thrives excellently at our latitudes. Don't apply the oil before sunbathing.
Effects: alleviates pain, excitatory, improves circulation, antiseptic, improves skin issues, cleanses the blood
Yield: 0.4–3 percent

Lime
(Citrus aurantifolia, C. limetta)

You can use lime peels the same way described for lemons. Don't use the oil in direct sunlight.
Effects: deodorant, antiseptic, invigorating, exhilarating
Yield: 5–7 percent

Lovage
(Ligusticum levisticum)

Both the roots and the leaves contain essential oil. You can use fresh, dried, or fermented roots, but don't forget to chop them up. Distill the leaves fresh.
Effects: helps with digestive issues and mucus congestion in the stomach as well as kidney diseases
Yield: leaves: 0.3–0.5 percent; roots: 0.3–1.0 percent

Marigold
(Calendula officinalis, Tagetes patula, T. tenuifolia)

Common marigold, pot marigold, or garden marigold (*Calendula officinalis*) is well-established in herbal medicine, especially for body and massage oils. Popular herbal and cosmetic products named calendula invariably derive from *C. officinalis*. Naturalized in large parts of Europe and North America, the marigold is presumed to have originated in the Mediterranean. The essential oil is made from the flowers. Collect flower heads that have not yet opened. The best time to pick them is June through September.

French marigold (*Tagetes patula*) is the best-known cultivar of the genus Tagetes, which is native to the Americas and naturalized around the world. *T. patula* is mainly used as an edging plant on herbaceous borders. New varieties and hybrids unfortunately do not contain any essential oil because the strong smell of the leaves is undesirable (even though it's a repellant against pests like whiteflies). However, to obtain essential oil from the original *T. patula*, cut up the entire plant and distill it when in flower. The oil is blended with sandalwood oil to produce the attar genda perfume.

Signet marigold or yellow/orange gem marigold (*Tagetes tenuifolia*) provides an especially beautiful, dark red, bitter-spicy oil. Cut up the whole plant after it blooms and distill it.
Effects: Calendula: relieves cramps, induces sweating, relieves pain. Tagetes: antiseptic, calming, antifungal (e.g., treatment of candidiasis)
Yield: calendula: 0.1 percent, tagetes: 0.5–1 percent

▲ Blooming signet marigold (orange gem marigold)

Marjoram
(Origanum majorana)

Cut up and distill the ends and leaves of the herb when it's blooming. Oil made from fresh herbs will have a greenish color, and oil made from dried herbs will be yellowish. If it's stored under cool conditions, hard crystals known as marjoram stearoptenes will form. Don't use products from marjoram oil on your face.
Effects: alleviates bronchitis and rheumatism, relieves cramps, relaxant
Yield: fresh: 0.3–0.4 percent; dried: 0.7–0.9 percent

Mint: spearmint, pennyroyal, field mint, peppermint
(Mentha spicata, M. viridis, var. crispa, var. nanah, M. pulegium, M. arvensis, M. piperita, M. canadensis)

There are many cultivated varieties of mint. Some that are relevant for oil production are spearmint (*M. spicata, M. viridis*) and peppermint (*M. piperita*). All types of mint oil can be extracted via steam distillation due to their relatively high oil contents. The spearmint category includes curled mint (*var. crispa*) and Nana mint (*var. nanah*), among others. Unlike peppermint oil, spearmint oil does not contain any menthol and thus has no cooling effect. Fresh, blooming curled mint provides more oil than when it's dried. The quality of the oil can be improved by just using the leaves and tips of the stems. Nana mint is a Moroccan variety of the (European) curled mint.

Spearmint produces an oil commonly used in chewing gum, toothpaste, and other products. The best way to obtain it is to distill fresh blossoms (though you can also use the whole herb).

▲ Japanese peppermint oil

The American wild mint (*M. arvensis villosa*, synonym: *M. canadensis*) is used as an insect repellent and in homes as a strewing herb to keep rodents away. The essential oil is obtained from the leaves; it is used as a flavoring for toothpastes and such.

You can get the best possible peppermint oil by distilling only the leaves while the plant is in bloom. This is another case where fresh herbs produce more oil than dried ones, but oil made from dried herbs has a longer shelf life because sticky volatile components turn to resin during the drying process and are thus not distilled. Harvest the mint in September during the midday heat, when you can see a red grid pattern on the leaves. You can harvest from the same plant for multiple years, but it will provide the best results in the second year. During the distillation, you should make sure to separate the later fractions from the first ones, which will have a finer fragrance.

Japanese peppermint oil (*M. arvensis var. piperescens*), on the other hand, is generally made exclusively from dried herbs. It will either already be congealed at room temperature or long, stick-like menthol crystals (peppermint stearoptenes) will form at around 53°F–59°F (12°C–15°C). This oil, or the menthol extracted from it, makes up part of the famous Tiger Balm.

Warning: Only use peppermint at low concentrations or skin irritation may result.

Effects: alleviates headaches as well as respiratory and digestive issues, antiseptic

Yield: mint: 0.2–0.4 percent; peppermint, fresh: 0.1–0.3 percent, dried: 0.5–1.5 percent

Mountain pine
(Pinus mugo subsp. mugo)

The harvest time and production process are the same as for the spruce. Commerically, the oil is usually produced from the needles.
Effects: antiseptic, dissolves mucus, relieves colds and rheumatism, improves circulation
Yield: 0.1–0.7 percent

Mugwort

See wormwood.

Myrrh
(Commiphora myrrha)

The oil is extracted from the myrrh bush's resin via alcoholic extraction.
Effects: anti-inflammatory, remedies hemorrhoids, slows skin aging
Yield: 2–10 percent

Myrtle
(Myrtus communis)

Use the blooming flowers, fresh leaves, and twigs between June and August.
Effects: calming, antiseptic, alleviates respiratory issues, clarifying, soothes the skin
Yield: 0.1–0.6 percent

Narcissus
(Narcissus poeticus)

The oil is produced from the white blossoms via enfleurage or solvent extraction.
Effects: calming, relaxant
Yield: 0.06–0.1 percent

Nutmeg
(Myristica fragrans)

It's especially important to chop up nutmeg thoroughly before you distill it. If you grind the seeds, place a coffee filter or a cloth on the steamer basket to keep the fine particles from burning in the kettle. Only use the oil externally.
Effects: stimulant, relaxant, moderates intestinal issues
Yield: 8–15 percent

Oakmoss
(Evernia, Parmelia, Ramalina, Usnea)

Collect moss from trees before the leaves sprout, in the winter or early spring. The oil is extracted via solvent extraction or enfleurage.
Effects: light aphrodisiac, relaxant
Yield: 0.01–0.1 percent

Orange
(Citrus aurantium dulcis, C. sinensis, C. sinensis moro)

The same applies to the orange as to the lemon; you can find a detailed description in its section. Instead of cold pressing or distilling fresh peels, you can also dry the peels and then distill them.
You can get three different types of oil from the orange tree.
Orange oil from the orange zest
Petitgrain oil, which can be distilled from the leaves, twigs, and unripe fruits.
Neroli oil, which can be distilled from the blossoms; pick them in early May. The hydrosol produced from this distillation is called orange flower water. It smells completely different from

▲ Orange

and much more subtle than neroli oil because orange blossoms contain both a water-soluble and a water-insoluble odorant. Only the water-soluble one is contained in the hydrosol. Fake "orange flower water" is often produced by shaking neroli oil, but it smells like the oil and not like the real hydrosol, making it relatively simple to distinguish fakes. The chemical properties are also different.
Effects: soothes the skin, alleviates colds, exhilarating, harmonizing, purifying, strengthens tissue (e.g., in cases of cellulitis)
Yield: fruits: 0.4–2.5 percent; blossoms: 0.1 percent

Oregano
(Origanum vulgare)

Distill fresh or dried leaves and stem tips, use the plants while they're blooming.
Effects: antiseptic, appetite stimulant, strengthens the stomach, improves circulation
Yield: 0.1–0.3 percent

Palmarosa
(Cymbopogon martinii, Andropogon schoenanthus)

Use fresh stalks and blossoms of this tropical grass. Its fragrance is similar to that of rose oil, so palmarosa oil is often used to dilute it.
Effects: antiseptic, soothes the skin, deodorant
Yield: 1–2 percent

Palo santo
(Bursera graveolens)

Chop up the wood of this balsa tree well and distill it. Palo santo incense has a high essential oil concentration.
Effects: warming, causes euphoria, germicidal, builds resistance
Yield: 0.8–2 percent

Parsley
(Apium petroselinum)

Distill both ripe seeds and well-cut-up blossom tips and leaves. They should be collected in September. Oil distilled from the roots has a less distinctive parsley fragrance than oil made from the leaves. Parsley oil is heavier than water, so it collects at the bottom of the receiver container.
Effects: alleviates urinary diseases
Yield: herb: 0.02–0.08 percent; seeds: 2.0–6.0 percent

Patchouli
(Pogostemon cablin, P. patchouli)

Dry the brown-black leaves and small blossoms of the patchouli bush and, for the typical aroma, ferment them a little like black tea, then distill them.

The various types of patchouli can only be cultivated in pots at our latitudes at temperatures over 54°F (12°C). Patchouli oil is produced commercially in India and Java. The Javanese oil is inferior because Indian patchouli has a much lovelier, sweeter aroma. When added after being heavily diluted, this oil reinforces the scents of other odorants, accentuating them to a degree. Its quality improves over the years if you store it. Patchouli, in woody, oriental compositions, is an indispensable part of classic perfumery.

Effects: antiseptic, soothes the skin, relaxant, aphrodisiac
Yield: 1.5–4.0 percent

Harvest the green, unripe berries in the afternoon. Crush fresh or dried peppercorns with a mortar and pestle and then distill them. The still-unripe berries of both green and black pepper should be dried, but black pepper berries have to ferment for a few days first. Initially, the fragrance of green pepper oil is more pleasant and subtle than that of black pepper oil, which smells like fish at first but then develops a very fine scent after being stored for six to twelve months.
    Don't use the oil on your face.
Effects: stimulant, relieves joint and muscle pain
Yield: 1–2 percent

Pepper
(Piper nigrum)

See mint.

Peppermint

Use dried carrot seeds. They should be harvested in September.
Effects: relieves stress, relaxant
Yield: 0.8–1.6 percent

Queen Anne's lace (wild carrot)
(Daucus carota)

Use fresh chopped up ramson leaves. Warning: Don't confuse them with lilies of the valley or arum leaves when you pick them.
Effects: stimulant, detoxifying, blood purifying, antihypertensive
Yield: 0.01–0.05 percent

Ramson
(Allium ursinum)

Use the shrub's sticky leaves and branches.
Effects: helps with skin disease, helps wounds heal, antiseptic, relieves cramps, stimulant, relaxant
Yield: 1–1.5 percent

Rockrose
(Cistus ladanifer)

The best roses for producing rose oil are the Damascus rose from Turkey and Bulgaria and the apothecary's rose from France. Only old varieties of roses are suitable for oil production; new varieties no longer contain any oil. Double distilling is necessary due to the low oil yield (about 11,000 pounds [5,000 kilograms] of rose petals are needed to produce 1 quart [1 liter] of oil). A small amount of oil will appear after the first distillation, but it has a different chemical composition from the oil produced during the second distillation. The familiar rose oil and rosewater won't appear until after both distillations are complete. In commercial production, the hydrosol from the first distillation is the only thing that's distilled in the second distillation.
    It's very important to pick roses at the right time. They should be picked between 4 and 5 a.m., during sunrise. For the best possible quality and yield, you should only pick complete, fully bloomed

Rose
(Rosa damascene, R. gallica, R. alba, R. centifolia)

▲ Rose balm blossom

Damascus rose ▶

rose petals directly underneath the flower head. If they're already withering, it's too late. Afterward, distill as soon as possible. Even storing the petals for just a few hours can lead to serious losses in quality and yield as fermentation starts to take place.
Effects: suitable for all skin types, anti-inflammatory, antidepressant, aphrodisiac, cleansing, strengthening, helps during childbirth, can be used in baby care
Yield: 0.02–0.03 percent

Rosemary
(Rosmarinus officinalis)

Distill its cut-up leaves, twigs, and flower heads (take heed of the note on page 43). They should be collected between May and August. You can then use the herb either fresh or dried.
Effects: improves circulation, calms the nerves, raises blood pressure, reduces fatigue, stimulates the brain, alleviates respiratory issues, invigorates the skin and hair (intensifies growth)
Yield: 1–2 percent

Rosewood
(Aniba rosaeodora)

Chop up branches and leaves of the rosewood tree well and distill them. Only use the oil externally.
Effects: antibacterial, relaxant, soothes the skin, reduces anxiety and fatigue
Yield: 0.8–1.2 percent

Rue
(Ruta graveolens)

This herb is a classic ingredient in grappa (*grappa di ruta*) and has its own spicy scent, as does its essential oil. Small amounts of it are used as a spice or perfume. You can extract the oil by cutting up the herb while it's blooming and then distilling it while it's fresh. It is harvested in July and August during the heat of the day, as always with herbs. There are countless stories, some of them magical, surrounding this plant, which was already very well-known in the ancient world, where it was used in conventional and folk medicine. However, it's not a good idea to use it therapeutically today because both the herb and its oil have toxic side effects (irritation of the skin and mucus membranes, especially in sunlight, intestinal irritation, risk of triggering a miscarriage, fertility reduction, a mild narcotic effect, etc.). Because of these risks, adding rue oil to perfumes or similar products at concentrations greater than 3.9 percent is prohibited. A major component of the oil, methyl nonyl ketone or "rue ketone," is an active ingredient in dog and cat repellants because pets cannot stand its smell.

▲ Blooming sage

Effects: at low doses, physical and appetite stimulant; helps against headaches, vertigo, colic, digestive issues, and problems urinating; increases sweat production
Yield: 0.15–0.18 percent

Sage
(Salvia officinalis)

Distill the leaves, either fresh or dried. They should be picked in July or August, while the sage is in bloom.
Effects: darkens hair, anti-inflammatory, relieves pain, relieves cramps, lowers blood pressure, purifies the blood, inhibits sweating
Yield: 1.5–2.5 percent

Sandalwood, amyris
(Santalum album, Amyris balsamifera)

Chop up the branches and yellow wood well and then distill them. Don't harvest a tree until it's at least forty years old. Amyris is a West Indian variety of the East Indian sandalwood, but of far lesser quality.
Effects: soothes the skin, alleviates respiratory issues, antidepressant, antiseptic, relieves cramps, anti-inflammatory, calming
Yield: 3–5 percent

Savory
(Satureja hortensis, S. montana)

Cut up the whole herb (fresh or dried) and place it in the kettle. Florists sell special varieties that can produce oil yields of up to 4 percent.
Effects: relieves cramps, appetite stimulant, antiseptic, invigorating, helps your skin, deodorant, relaxant
Yield: 0.1–1 percent

▲ Scotch pine with young cones

Scotch pine
(Pinus sylvestris)

You can chop up and distill the needles, the twigs, and the cones. Collect them between May and August; this is when the plants contain the highest oil content.
Effects: alleviates coughing, bronchitis, and respiratory infections
Yield: 0.4–0.5 percent

Spike lavender See lavender.

Spikenard See valerian.

**Spruce,
Norway spruce**
(Picea abies)
You can chop up and distill the needles, the twigs, and the cones. Collect them between May and August; this is when the plants contain the highest oil content.
Effects: antiseptic, deodorant, stimulates breathing, relaxant
Yield: 0.5–1 percent

St. John's wort
(Hypericum perforatum)
Chop and distill the whole herb. Harvest the plant between mid-June and the end of August during the midday heat. St. John's wort used to only be picked on the feast day of St. John, June 24.
Effects: improves your mood, antidepressant, alleviates rheumatism, relieves cramps, strengthens the nerves
Yield: 0.05–0.1 percent

**Strawflower,
immortelle,
everlasting**
(Helichrysum italicum)
You can produce oil from either the blossoms of this wildflower or by cutting up whole, blooming plants.
Effects: anti-inflammatory, tightens tissue, detoxifying, relieves vein issues
Yield: 1–1.3 percent

Swiss pine
(Pinus cembra)
The harvest time and production process are the same as for the spruce. In commercial operations, the needles are usually the only part that's used.
Effects: improves circulation, alleviates rheumatism as well as skin problems and coughing
Yield: 0.4–0.6 percent

Tangerine
(Citrus reticulata, C. nobilis)
The same goes as for the lemon. Tangerine oil has almost the exact same characteristics as orange oil but is significantly milder.
Effects: invigorating and stimulating, relaxant, antidepressant, appetite stimulant, antiseptic
Yield: 0.7–2 percent

Tansy
(Tanacetum vulgare)
Cut up the fresh herbs and distill them as soon as the flower heads have fully formed.
Effects: relieves cramps, can be used as an insecticide
Yield: 0.2–0.3 percent

Tarragon
(Artemisia dracunculus)
Harvest the entire herb when it's blooming at the end of the summer or early in fall.
Effects: strengthens the stomach, appetite stimulant, strengthens you, invigorating, alleviates rheumatism, improves circulation
Yield: 0.1–0.4 percent

Tea tree
(Melaleuca alternifolia)

The leaves and twigs of the tea tree are used. Tea tree oil should be diluted with a carrier oil (see chapter 5) before being applied to the skin or it may cause irritation.
Effects: kills germs in wounds and colds, alleviates pain, strengthening
Yield: 1–2 percent

Thuja
(Thuja occidentalis, T. plicata)

The thuja, or arborvitae, is found in hedge form in almost every garden. Thoroughly chop up and then distill the tips of its branches. This is a way to put your yard waste to good use, and your neighbors will surely also be happy to see you prune their thuja hedges on your side a little. Collect the twigs and leaves between May and October. Thuja oil has a very refreshing fragrance. The oil should only be used externally because about 50–60 percent of it consists of thujone.
Effects: excellent against warts
Yield: 1–1.6 percent

Thyme, wild thyme/creeping thyme
(Thymus vulgaris, T. officinalis, T. serpyllum)

Harvest the blooming ends of the herb in midsummer, then cut them up and distill them directly. You can also dry them without any issues. Interestingly, different stills produce differently colored oil: copper stills produce red oil, whereas stainless steel stills produce colorless oil.

Wild thyme oil (*T. serpyllum*) is usually made by cutting up the whole herb fresh while it's in bloom and distilling, but you can also use it dried.
Effects: Thyme: calming, dehydrating, digestive, reduces fevers, appetite stimulant, improves circulation, strengthens the nerves, invigorating, helps with wound healing and respiratory illnesses
Wild thyme: alleviates coughing and pain, digestive, antiseptic, helps with stomach and digestive illnesses, trouble sleeping, and headaches, can be used externally against rheumatism
Yield: Thyme: 0.7–5 percent, wild thyme: 0.4–0.6 percent

Tuberose, night hyacinth
(Polianthes tuberosa)

Because white tuberose blossoms give off their scent mostly in the evening and at night, the plant is also known as the night hyacinth. The oil from these blossoms is one of the most expensive types and is extracted via enfleurage or solvent extraction.
Effects: relaxant, sensual, aphrodisiac
Yield: 0.05–0.1 percent

Turmeric
(Curcuma longa)

This plant belongs to the ginger family. Distill the roots after drying them and chopping them up.
Effects: improves circulation, stimulates digestion
Yield: 4.5–5.5 percent

Valerian, Alpine valerian, spikenard
(Valeriana officinalis, Valeriana celtica ssp. Norica, *Nardostachys jatamansi* Valerianaceae)

▲ Alpine valerian after blooming (top), leaves and roots (bottom)

The root is the only part of the valerian plant (*Valeriana officinalis*) that can be distilled. The plant should be at least two to three years old, at which point the root can be harvested in fall. You can also dry the root: cut it up and leave it in the sun, or you can help it along by putting it in the oven at a maximum of 158°F (70°C). The typical scent of valerian, which magically attracts cats, is particularly strong while it's drying. This scent is equally attractive to rats, therefore valerian roots are often used by rat-catchers to bait their traps. According to recent research, valerian root is also the strongest chemoattractant of slime molds (*Physarum polycephalum*).

The Alpine valerian (*Valeriana celtica* ssp. norica), also known as celtic valerian, valerian spikenard, or Alpine spikenard, grows at elevations of over 6,500 feet (2,000 meters) in the Tauern region of southern Austria and is protected by strict conservation measures. Only a small number of farmers are permitted to harvest Alpine valerian, despite the fact that it's been scientifically proven that the plant spreads farther if about half of the field it's growing in is harvested each year. Before it became illegal to harvest it, Alpine valerian played a large role in folk medicine and was traded as far away as Egypt about 2,500 years ago. There, it was used as a base material for perfumes. Its essential oil is extracted from dried roots. Fresh roots also contain oil, but the fragrance is much better if distilled from the dried roots. Harvest the roots between mid-August and mid-September. Like with true valerian, the smell of fresh Alpine valerian roots left out to dry is extremely attractive to cats.

Spikenard (*Nardostachys jatamansi* Valerianaceae) is a flowering plant of the Valerian family that grows in the Himalayas of Nepal, India, Bhutan, and Tibet. The plant is found at altitudes of about 10,000–16,500 feet (3,000–5,000 meters). Chop up and distill the dried roots. Unlike true valerian, spikenard has a pleasant scent. Spikenard oil was the most precious and expensive perfume in the ancient world, only available to priests, kings, and high-level initiates. Mary Magdalene anointed Jesus's feet with it, and it was also found in King Tut's tomb. The scent of spikenard also attracts cats.

Effects: Valerian: alleviates stomach and intestinal issues, aids sleep, calming. Alpine valerian: relieves cramps, lowers fevers, stimulates circulation, strengthens the stomach. Spikenard: good for the skin, relaxant, relieves stress, improves circulation, strengthens the cardiovascular system, anti-inflammatory, relieves itching, stimulates pheromone production

Yield: Valerian: 0.2–1.0 percent, alpine valerian: 0.5–1.5 percent, spikenard: 0.25–0.5 percent

Vetiver
(*Vetiveria zizanioides, Andropogon muricatus*)

This plant is related to lemongrass. The roots are dried and distilled.
Effects: strengthens the nerves, soothes the skin, relaxant, improves circulation, induces sweating
Yield: 0.4–0.9 percent

Violet
(*Viola odorata*)

Collect violet leaves in March and April. The oil is extracted via solvent extraction or enfleurage.
Effects: alleviates nervousness and insomnia as well as headaches, strengthens the nerves
Yield: 0.04 percent

Wattle, mimosa
(*Acacia decurrens, A. dealbata*)

Mimosa oil is extracted from the blossoms and twig ends. Commercially it is produced via solvent extraction, but some users have been successful with enfleurage. The absolute and concrete are used as a fixative in soaps and fragrance for superior-grade perfumery. Another use is aromatherapy.
Effects: helps you sleep, reduces fear and anxiety
Yield: 0.3–0.7 percent

Wormwood, mugwort
(*Artemisia absinthium, A. vulgaris, Absinthii herba*)

Wormwood (*A. absinthium* or *Absinthii herba*) is also known as absinthium, absinthe wormwood, or green ginger. Chop up and distill the ends of the branches when the plant is blooming. Usually fresh herbs are used, but dried ones can be distilled, too. The oil has a dark blue-green color. It's made up largely of thujone, the active ingredient in absinthe. Absinthe was banned for decades in many countries due to this substance. However, it's become legal to sell it again during the last few years, as long as it doesn't exceed a certain thujone content. In high doses, thujone is a neurotoxin and supposedly has intoxicating effects.

From the mugwort or common wormwood (*Artemisia vulgaris*) collect twigs along with leaves and blossoms in August and roots in the fall. You should dry the roots quickly to avoid losing some of the oil.
Effects: Wormwood: alleviates stomach problems, appetite stimulant. Mugwort: alleviates pain from menstrual and other cramps, diuretic
Yield: Wormwood: 0.2–0.4 percent, mugwort: leaves: 0.03–0.2 percent; roots: 0.05–0.1 percent

Yarrow
(*Achillea millefolium*)

This plant is a great choice for a first attempt because it grows almost everywhere. Distill the cut-up flower heads. It's best to pick them on a sunny day between the beginning of July and mid-September. The oil appears dark blue because it contains the ingredient chamazulene, much like chamomile oil, which contains the same substance.

Effects: improves circulation, anti-inflammatory, stimulant, relieves cramps
Yield: 0.2–0.5 percent

Yellow jade orchid blossoms, champaca, Joy *(Magnolia champaca, Michelia champaca* L.*)*

Joy, one of the most expensive perfume fragrances in the world, is made from champaca trees. In Southeast Asia, their blossoms are used in ceremonies, massages, Ayurvedic recipes, and to flavor tea. For example, a blossom can be placed in water, which is then sprinkled onto things. The scent of a single blossom can be perceived several hundred meters away—it's enough to serve as an air freshener for an entire room. The plant grows well in pots in our part of the world, in which case the blossoms should be harvested in May and June. As with roses or jasmine, pick them early in the morning.

Due to the small amounts of oil produced, enfleurage or extraction are also reasonable options along with distillation. Depending on the type, champaca trees have white or yellow blossoms. Either can be used to produce oil, but only the yellow blossoms give you the "true" champaca oil. Use the blossoms immediately after picking them or they will turn brown and lose their scent.

Effects: calming, relaxant, aphrodisiac, diuretic
Yield: 0.01–0.05 percent

Ylang-ylang/ cananga *(Cananga odorata)*

Ylang-ylang and cananga oil are extracted via distillation from the fresh yellow blossoms of two subspecies of the western Pacific ylang-ylang or cananga tree, which is related to anemones. Cut the blossoms early in the morning. The entire ylang-ylang oil is always used in aromatherapy.

For other products, fractional distilling is used to produce oil of varying qualities. The components are removed from the plant material in order of their volatility. Fractioning and/or varying the distillation time can thus be used to accumulate the most desirable components. Four distinct fractions are partitioned during distillation and are referred to as "extra," "I," "II," and "III." The liquids range from pale yellow to deep yellow, with a characteristic flowery, spicy, balsamic scent. The composition of the fractions depends on how long the distillation went on. The first two fractions are the most valuable: the "extra" fraction has the highest concentration of components with strongly intense fragrances. Ylang-ylang "extra" and "I" are generally used in fine fragrance mixtures, while ylang-ylang "II" and "III" are used to give fragrance to soap.

Considering the distillation methods used with ylang-ylang, it's no surprise that its oil is available in different qualities. During a one-to-two-day distillation with a 300-to-500-liter still, the hydrosol is continually recirculated back into the kettle by an overflow pipe, which inevitably results in overcooking and a worsening smell. If you distill ylang-ylang blossoms exactly as described starting on page 42, however, you'll get oil of the highest quality, even in the third hydrosol bottle.

Effects: lowers blood pressure, calming, slows your heart rate, aphrodisiac, clears the skin (greasy skin)

Yield: 1.5–2.5 percent

Overview: Plants and their effects

We'll conclude the chapter with an overview of all the plants and their effects once again. Please keep in mind that you should consult with a doctor or other health care professional before ingesting pure essential oils or hydrosols. The same goes for the appropriate concentration and method of usage, such as in fragrant oil burners, wet packs, massage oils, aroma baths, steam baths, steam inhalations, etc.

Ailment	Plant
Acne	Chamomile, lavender, myrrh, peppermint, thyme, juniper, lemon
Anxiety	Geranium, chamomile, marjoram, lemon balm, orange, rose, juniper
Bronchitis	Eucalyptus, chamomile, myrtle, peppermint, rosemary, thyme
Cellulite	Geranium, mint, myrtle, orange, oregano, rose, rosemary, sage, juniper, lemon
Depression	Basil, geranium, jasmine, chamomile, lavender, lemon balm, rose
Diarrhea	Eucalyptus, geranium, chamomile, lavender, oregano, peppermint, rosemary
Difficulty concentrating	Basil, geranium, bay leaf, marjoram, mint, rosemary, fir, thyme, juniper, lemon, cypress
Digestive issues	Anise, basil, fennel, ginger, chamomile, cilantro, lavender, bay leaf, lemon balm, clove, peppermint
Fatigue	Camphor, mint, rosemary, juniper, cypress
Hair loss	Birch, rosemary, thyme
Headache	Chamomile, lavender, peppermint, rose, rosemary
High blood pressure	Lavender, marjoram, lemon balm, orange, ylang-ylang
Insect bites	Lavender, tea tree

◂ Which plants help with which ailments?

Low blood pressure	Eucalyptus, peppermint, rosemary, sage, thyme, juniper, hyssop
Menstrual issues	Jasmine, chamomile, lavender, lemon balm, marjoram, rose, sage, juniper
Nervousness	Jasmine, chamomile, lavender, lemon balm, rose, sage
Rheumatism	Eucalyptus, spruce, chamomile, lavender, marjoram, rosemary, thyme, juniper
Sleep disorders	Jasmine, chamomile, lavender, marjoram, rose
Stomach issues	Basil, fennel, geranium, ginger, chamomile, lavender, lemon balm, sage
Stress	Basil, geranium, lavender, tea tree

A small collection of home-distilled essential oils ▶

CHAPTER 5

Using Your Oils

Now that you're familiar with how essential oils and hydrosols are produced, this chapter will provide you with basic recipes for how to use your homemade oils and herbal waters.

The recipes use dosages of essential oils that ensure that the products won't have a single dominant scent. You can, of course, always use more or less of the given oils to suit your personal taste. It's also possible to mix multiple oils instead of just using a single one—we leave this entirely up to your imagination.

Before we move on to the individual recipes, the next few pages will give you a general overview of which oils are especially suitable for which products. The table will also serve as a foundation for the subsequent recipes. You can always refer to this table to select an appropriate oil.

Some explanation is needed before we go on to the recipes.

Base substances and materials

Many recipes involve a neutral carrier oil. When buying one, make sure that you're actually getting a natural product. The following mild vegetable oils are possibilities for the carrier oil.

Almond oil: classic for massages, suitable for every skin type, light and mild, excellent with dry skin and wrinkles, shelf life of only two months

◀ Ingredients for scented soap: water, neutral carrier oil (thistle), beeswax, essential oil (anise), and odorless soap flakes. Recipe on page 109.

Avocado oil: absorbed well by the skin without leaving a greasy film behind, has a nourishing effect (for dry and mature skin), contains vitamins and lecithin

Corn oil: especially appropriate for mature skin, helps the skin regenerate by including vitamin A

Jojoba oil: nurses, protects, and regulates the skin's moisture balance; contains vitamin E; doesn't leave behind grease, making it suitable for facial care; has a natural SPF of 3–4; fixes essential oils, making it also suitable for perfume production; shelf life of two to three years; neutral scent

Which essential oils are suitable for which products? ▶

Product	Plant
Bath additive	Mugwort, jasmine, lavender, mint, rose, marigold, rosemary, yarrow
Facial creams, lotions, massage oils, facial cleanser	Angelica, bergamot, fennel, geranium, jasmine, St. John's wort, chamomile, cilantro, lavender, bitter orange, orange, marigold, rose, rosemary, yarrow, tea tree, thyme, violet, ylang-ylang, lemon
Footbath	Mugwort, rosemary, sage, lemon, cypress
Fragrant oil burner	Fig, grapefruit, mountain pine, orange, fir, lemon
Gauze pads	Lavender, orange, rose
Hair care	Bergamot, birch, citronella, chamomile, lavender, rosewood, rosemary, sage, thyme, cedar, lemon
Perfume	Basil, geranium, spiced oils, ginger, jasmine, magnolia, needle oils, bitter orange, patchouli, rose, rosewood, rosemary, sandalwood, violet, cinnamon, lemon balm
Sauna infusions	Cajuput, vervain, eucalyptus, spruce, pine, lemon balm, mint, myrtle, bitter orange, petitgrain, peppermint, rosemary, fir, tea tree, juniper, cedar, cedarwood, lemon, cypress
Soap	Lavender, mint, rose, marigold, rosemary, thyme, violet

Note: Place a drop of essential oil on the back of your hand or the crook of your arm. If the skin quickly becomes irritated, you should avoid that type of oil.

Note: Only make as much of a product as you need. Once an essential oil has been diluted, it can go rancid after just a few months.

Macadamia oil: nurses, smoothes, and nourishes the skin; has a natural SPF of 3–4; contains vitamins (A, B, C, D, and E) and minerals; has a lightly nutty scent

Olive oil: especially good for foot and nail care, has its own strong scent

Sesame oil: healing, detoxifying, and warming, contains a high amount of essential fatty acids, prevents oxidation and absorbs UV radiation (good sun protection)

Soy oil: very fatty and rich in nutrients

Sunflower oil: good with unclean and greasy skin

Walnut oil: for all skin types

Wheat germ oil: invigorating and has a regenerative effect; strengthens healing power; contains vitamins, lecithin, enzymes, and linoleic acid; long shelf life; has a relatively strong scent of its own; usually just used to enrich other carrier oils

Note: Any carrier oil can be combined with any essential oil.

The following additives also appear in the recipes.

Additives

Alcohol: Use non-denatured, high-percentage (greater than 80 percent ABV) alcohol (i.e., ethanol). It should definitely not be denatured or else the toxin that makes the rectified spirit undrinkable will get on your skin, plus it has a penetrating scent. In the perfume industry, a substance is used to denature alcohol that gives many people an allergic reaction. In our experience so far, nobody who experiences allergic reactions to regular perfumes has had a reaction to homemade products. But this is not a scientifically valid field study, of course. If you have any interest in distilling schnapps, it's not too difficult to make this base substance yourself.

Beeswax: from the honeycombs in beehives, solidifies creams

Hydrosol: Many of the recipes recommend adding the hydrosol, especially for the following types of oil: chamomile, cypress, eucalyptus, fennel, lavender, lemon balm, mint, myrtle, orange blossom, peppermint, rockrose, rose, rosemary, sage, sandalwood, tea tree, thyme, and vervain.

You can also use the hydrosol in place of water in the recipes, as it contains lots of valuable and fragrant substances. Don't boil it, however, or the oils in the water will be destroyed and may even cause an unpleasant scent to form.

With hydrosols it will be clearly evident if the producer is focused solely on essential oils. We once bought some rose geranium water from which we could hardly recognize any kind of odor. However, this clear, colorless, and nearly odorless liquid was not at all comparable with our own hydrosol. We roughly estimated that the purchased product was diluted 1:20 or even more.

Lanolin (wool fat): extracted from sheep's wool, helps to keep the water-oil mixture stable (emulsifier).

Soap flakes: you can either make them from perfume-free soap or buy pre-made soap flakes at a health food store.

Soft soap: the active detergent in shower gel, for example, available in pharmacies and health food stores in the form of a tough paste.

Shaking the hydrosol

Making your own hydrosol: Mix about 3 milliliters of essential oil with 1 quart (1 liter) of water.

Take equal amounts of the hydrosol and a neutral carrier oil. Shake them together thoroughly in a separatory funnel (see page 50) and let the mixture sit for about half an hour. Repeat this process three or four times. Then you can separate the watery layer using the outflow valve. The carrier oil will have absorbed the essential oil from the hydrosol because the essential oil is much more soluble in it than in water. This oil can then be used directly in massages or as a facial oil, or you can use it as a starting product in one of the recipes.

Equipment

You'll need the following equipment to make the different products:

Beaker glass: to heat the carrier oil, water, etc., in a water bath and to mix different ingredients

Letter scale or kitchen scale: to precisely measure out quantities

Stove top: to heat the water bath

Wooden spatula: to stir and blend mixtures, especially important for creams

Pot: filled with water to function as a water bath

Note: A drop from a dropper is about 0.05 milliliters while a drop from a syringe with a needle is only about 0.014 milliliters.

Pasteur pipette or syringe with hypodermic needle: to place drops of essential oil. Keep in mind that drops from different pieces of equipment aren't always the same size: drops from a thick hypodermic needle or glass Pasteur pipette (see page 49) are only about a quarter to a third as large as drops from other pipettes, syringes with no needle, or the droppers that are often attached to essential oil bottles. In the recipes, the specified numbers of drops are for droppers, thus large drops. Therefore, if you use a thick needle or a glass Pasteur pipette, you'll have to use three to four times as many drops as are given in the recipes.

Safety precautions

Essential oils contain highly concentrated active ingredients and can sometimes be toxic in their undiluted forms, so you should always stick to a few guidelines:
- Keep your essential oils safely away from children.
- Don't rub essential oils into your eyes.
- Only use diluted essential oils on your skin—never on mucous membranes.
- Don't take pure essential oils internally without knowledge of the effects or the consultation of a professional practitioner.
- Essential oils are very potent substances. Don't use too much.
- The following oils increase the skin's light sensitivity and should not be added to skin oils that will be exposed to sunlight or UV radiation: pressed citrus oil, angelica root, and caraway.
- If you have sensitive skin, you should use the following oils only sparingly: angelica root, anise, basil, cajuput, cardamom, cilantro, cinnamon, citrus oils, clove, eucalyptus, fennel, fir, ginger, jasmine, lemon balm, lemongrass, mint, neroli, oregano, pepper, savory, thyme, and vervain.
- If you're pregnant, you must not use the following oils (except after consulting with a doctor): anise, basil, bay leaf, camphor, cilantro, cinnamon, clary sage, clove, fennel, hyssop, juniper, lemon balm, marjoram, mint, myrrh, nutmeg, oregano, rockrose, rosemary, sage, savory, tarragon, and thyme.
- If you suffer from high blood pressure, you must not use the following oils (except after consulting with a doctor): bay leaf, hyssop, rosemary, sage, savory, and thyme.
- If you suffer from epilepsy, you must not use the following oils (except after consulting with a doctor): anise, basil, cypress, fennel, hyssop, lavandin, rosemary, and sage.

Bath additives

It's very easy to make bath additives. All you usually need is a pure essential oil and some kind of emulsifier like cream or milk to allow the oil to mix with water. Even easier is the usage of hydrosols: just pour them in the bathwater and stir.

Full bath additive

You need:
- 1 tablespoon of cream, milk, and honey
- 5–10 drops of essential oil

First dissolve a tablespoon of honey into the bathwater. Then mix the essential oil with the cream or milk and add it to the bathwater. The water temperature should not be above 100°F (38°C) or the oil will evaporate too quickly.

Hydrosols: depending on the distilled type of plant, use one up to three 6.8-fluid-ounce (200-milliliter) bottles (see section distilling in chapter 3).

Example: 5 drops of lavender oil (calming) or 5 drops of lavandin oil (invigorating) or 20 fluid ounces (600 milliliters) pure lavender/lavandin hydrosol

Bath salts

You need:
- 5.3 ounces (150 grams) of sea salt (for a full bath)
- 10–15 drops of essential oil

Place the perfume-free sea salt in a small container with a lid. Drip the oil evenly over the salt and then seal the container and shake it vigorously several times. After an hour, the bath salts will have fully absorbed the oil and will be ready to use.

Store-bought neutral sea salt is always colorless. If you wish to give your own bath salts a fitting color, however, doing so is relatively simple: buy some food coloring and mix it with water. About 10–20 drops of the diluted coloring is enough for half a cup or 5.3 ounces (150 grams) of salt—just spread it over the salt and then shake the salt vigorously inside a container. Then spread the salt on a paper and let it dry out overnight. Alternatively, leave it in the oven at 122°F (50°C) for half an hour. You should never add the essential oil until after the colored salt is dry.

Example: 10 drops of juniper oil

Bath salts ▶

Shower gel

Unlike the products just mentioned, this gel has a cleansing effect because it includes a substance with active detergent properties. It's best to use soft soap or silver soap (white soft soap) for this—for more lather, use more soft soap than listed in the recipe.

Heat the water or hydrosol to about 140°F (60°C) and dissolve the soft soap and honey in it while stirring. If you're also using vegetable oil, add it while stirring, too. Finally, stir in the vinegar. Don't add and stir in the essential oil until the mixture has cooled down to less than 86°F (30°C).

If you've used vegetable oil (the second recipe), two layers will form on their own after a while. You should therefore be sure to vigorously shake the mixture before you use it.

Example: 20 drops of orange oil, chamomile oil, or thyme oil. Hydrosol: mint, lemongrass, or bay (refreshing); rose, signet marigold, geranium (scented)

Footbath additive

First, dissolve the honey in the bathwater like with the full bath additive and then distribute the mixture of oil and milk or cream throughout the water. The water temperature should never exceed 100°F (38°C) in this case either.

Example: 7 drops of rosemary oil or 6.8 fluid ounces (200 milliliters) pure pine hydrosol

Facial and body care

For a full facial and body care regimen, you should make both cleansing and nurturing products. Each product's effects can be perfected by selecting the appropriate essential oils. You can always switch to adding different essential oils as the needs of your skin change. It's especially important to only use true essential oils here. Other fragrances may smell nice, but they'll have absolutely no effect on your skin.

You'll notice that all creams contain lanolin. Its job is to mix together the watery and fatty/oily portions of the cream and to prevent the aqueous and oily phase from separating again.

If you store your products under cool and dark conditions, they'll have a shelf life of two to three months.

Milky cleanser

Melt the beeswax and lanolin in a water bath and stir well. If you're adding a carrier oil, stir it in too and slowly add the water or hydrosol while still stirring. Let the mixture cool to a temperature of about 86°F (30°C) and then stir it more. Finally, add the drops of essential oil and stir well once again.

Depending on preference, you need:
- 3.5 ounces (100 grams) of soft soap
- 10 grams of honey
- 10 milliliters of fruit vinegar
- 6.8 fluid ounces (200 milliliters) of water
- 20 drops of essential oil

or
- 3.5 ounces (100 grams) of soft soap
- 10 grams of honey
- 10 milliliters of fruit vinegar
- 3.4 fluid ounces (100 milliliters) of water
- 3.4 fluid ounces (100 milliliters) of neutral carrier oil
- 20 drops of essential oil

You need:
- 1 tablespoon of cream, milk, and honey
- 3–7 drops of essential oil

Note: Facial care products should never have an essential oil content of more than 2 percent, while body care products should never exceed 3 percent.

You need:
- 8 grams of beeswax
- 10 grams of lanolin
- 3.4 fluid ounces (100 milliliters) of neutral carrier oil
- 3.4 fluid ounces (100 milliliters) of water or hydrosol
- 10 drops of essential oil

Example: Almond oil, 10 drops of lavender oil, and calendula hydrosol

Cleansing oil
Drip the essential oil into the carrier oil and thoroughly stir or shake them.
Example: Almond oil and 10 drops of rose oil

You need:
- 3.4 fluid ounces (100 milliliters) of neutral carrier oil
- 50 drops of essential oil

Makeup remover
Melt the beeswax in a water bath, slowly add the carrier oil, and mix them together well. Wait until the mixture has cooled to 86°F (30°C) and add the drops of essential oil. If you want to make the makeup remover runnier, don't use as much beeswax.
Example: Thistle oil and 3 drops of chamomile oil

You need:
- 10 grams of beeswax
- 1.7 fluid ounces (50 milliliters) of neutral carrier oil
- 3 drops of essential oil

Exfoliant (face scrub)
Melt the beeswax and lanolin in a water bath, slowly add the carrier oil, and mix it together and add the water or hydrosol while stirring. Wait for the mixture to cool to 86°F (30°C) and then add the drops of essential oil and stir in the salt. You should use the product within a week or the aqueous phase may partially separate from the mixture.
Example: 50 milliliters of almond oil, 3 drops of mint oil, and balm hydrosol.

You need:
- 10 grams of beeswax
- 5 grams of lanolin
- 1.7 fluid ounces (50 milliliters) of neutral carrier oil
- 1.7 fluid ounces (50 milliliters) of water
- 15–20 grams of salt
- 3 drops of essential oil

Face packs
Depending on your skin's particular characteristics, you can use a variety of different materials:
- *Egg yolk:* rejuvenates and smoothes
- *Egg white:* freshens tired skin
- *Oatmeal flakes:* cleans greasy skin
- *Medicinal clay:* for young skin
- *Honey:* for tightening and solidifying
- *Milk products:* stimulate cell growth
- *Wheat bran:* for unclean skin

You need:
- 3.4 fluid ounces (100 milliliters) of starting material
- 4–5 drops of essential oil

Use all of these materials directly, but mix the oatmeal flakes, medicinal clay, and wheat bran into a paste with water or hydrosol before adding the essential oil.

Facial cleanser
Add the drops of essential oil to the alcohol and then mix both of them well with water or hydrosol.

Alcohol-free facial cleansers are better for some skin types (alcohol dries out the skin a bit). In this case, use the second recipe. It's not absolutely necessary to add essential oils in either recipe if

With alcohol, you need:
- 3.0 fluid ounces (90 milliliters) of distilled water
- 10 milliliters of alcohol (96 percent ABV)
- 12 drops of essential oil

you use hydrosols instead of water. In this case the second recipe is pure hydrosol and nothing else.

As with all the other recipes, of course, you can also mix together different oils.

Example: 12 drops of lavender, peppermint, or carrot oil. Hydrosol: bay laurel, bay rum tree, or the same types as the oils

Without alcohol:
- 3.4 fluid ounces (100 milliliters) of distilled water
- 12 drops of essential oil

Facial cream

Melt the beeswax and lanolin in a water bath and add the carrier oil while stirring. Heat the hydrosol or distilled water to 140°F (60°C) and stir. Keep a close eye on the temperature or the components of the cream won't bind together! Add the drops of essential oil once the mixture has cooled to 86°F (30°C).

Only ever add the water or hydrosol to the carrier oil very slowly while you're stirring vigorously when you're making a cream. Be sure to keep stirring after it cools down or else the oil will mix poorly with the water, or won't mix at all, and the oil and water will immediately separate in the cream.

Pour the cream into a small container while it's lukewarm. After an hour, stir it again and seal the container. If you leave the cream standing longer, be sure to briefly stir it before you use it so it becomes soft and smooth again.

You need:
- 2 grams of beeswax
- 8 grams of lanolin
- 20 milliliters of neutral carrier oil
- 20 milliliters of hydrosol or distilled water
- 10–15 drops of essential oil

Variant: Heat the beeswax, cocoa butter, and lanolin to 140°F (60°C) in water bath—keep a close eye on this temperature. Stir in the carrier oil and heat the mixture back up to 140°F (60°C). Heat the hydrosol or distilled water to 140°F (60°C) as well and then slowly add it while stirring. Keep stirring until the mixture cools down to about 86°F (30°C) and then add the essential oil.

This cream should also be stirred before you use it if it's been sitting for a long time. It's very easy to alter the cream's composition:

- *Firmer cream:* use more beeswax
- *Softer cream:* use less beeswax
- *Lighter, thinner cream:* use more water/hydrosol
- *Richer, more fatty cream:* use more oil

For a different variant:
- 1.5 grams of beeswax
- 10 grams of lanolin
- 1.5 grams of cocoa butter
- 25 milliliters of neutral carrier oil
- 15 milliliters of hydrosol or distilled water
- 10–15 drops of essential oil

Example: 10 milliliters of almond or avocado oil, 20 milliliters of rose hydrosol, and 12 drops of lavender oil

Night cream

This type of cream is characterized by its lack of a watery component. This also makes it unnecessary to add the emulsifier lanolin.

Heat the carrier oil to 140°F (60°C) in a water bath and melt the wax in it. Then remove the mixture from the stove and add the drops of essential oil once it reaches 86°F (30°C).

You need:
- 2 grams of beeswax
- 40 milliliters of neutral carrier oil
- 10–15 drops of essential oil

Cream production

▲ Melt the beeswax and the lanolin in the water bath

▲ and stir in the oil.

Using Your Oils

▲ Slowly add the hydrosol or distilled water while stirring vigorously.

▲ Once the mixture has cooled down, you can add the drops of essential oil with the syringe and hypodermic needle.

For a more solid cream:
- 10 grams of beeswax
- 40 milliliters of neutral carrier oil
- 10–15 drops of essential oil

Heat the beeswax and carrier oil to 140°F (60°C) in a water bath and stir well. Stir in the essential oil once it's cooled to about 86°F (30°C).
Example: 20 milliliters of avocado oil, 20 milliliters of macadamia oil, and 14 drops of chamomile oil

Massage oil

You need:
- 3.4 fluid ounces (100 milliliters) of carrier oil
- 20–40 drops of essential oil

Mix the carrier oil with the essential oil.
Example: 50 milliliters of jojoba and almond oil, 20 drops of rosemary oil, and 20 drops of juniper oil

Facial oil

You need:
- 40 milliliters of neutral carrier oil
- 10–20 drops of essential oil

Add drops of the essential oil to the carrier oil and mix them.
Examples:
Almond oil and 15 drops of lavender oil
Jojoba oil and 20 drops of chamomile oil
Olive oil and 20 drops of carrot seed oil

Sunscreen oil

You need:
- 2.5 fluid ounces (75 milliliters) of sesame oil
- 5 teaspoons or 25 milliliters of wheat germ oil
- 4–8 drops of essential oil

These sunscreen oils aren't as effective as store-bought sunblocks, but they're excellent if you already have a tan.

Heat the carrier oils to 140°F (60°C) and mix them together well. Let it cool and then add the drops of essential oil.

You can also use 25 milliliters of coconut oil, 65 milliliters of sesame oil, and 10 milliliters of wheat germ oil instead of the given mixture of carrier oils.

Deodorant

You need:
- 1.7 fluid ounces (50 milliliters) of alcohol
- 20 drops of essential oil

Mix the ingredients together. You can refine the scent by also adding a couple of drops of lemon juice.
Example: 20 drops of sage oil

Mouthwash

You need:
- 6.8 fluid ounces (200 milliliters) of distilled water
- 1 teaspoon of alcohol (96 percent ABV)
- 8 drops of essential oil

First mix the essential oil with the alcohol and then add the water and stir it together. Alternatively use hydrosol instead of water, in this case essential oil is only necessary if the taste is too soft. If the taste of the hydrosol-alcohol-mixture is too strong, dilute it with water.
Example: 8 drops of peppermint oil or the same type of hydrosol

Shaving

Shaving soap
Heat the hydrosol to 140°F (60°C) and dissolve the soft soap in it. As soon as it's reached a lukewarm temperature, stir in the honey and the essential oil. Beating a teaspoon of the soap into a foam with water gives you enough to shave with. If you want it to be foamier, use more soft soap.
Example: 5 drops of bay leaf oil and calendula hydrosol

You need:
- 8.5 fluid ounces (250 milliliters) of hydrosol
- 50 grams of soft soap
- 1 teaspoon of honey
- 5 drops of essential oil

Aftershave
Depending on your preferences and skin type, you can make an aftershave with or mostly without alcohol to use after you shave.

First mix the essential oil with the alcohol and then add the water or hydrosol while stirring.
Example: 2 drops of vetiver oil, sandalwood hydrosol

You need:
- 6.8 fluid ounces (200 milliliters) of distilled water or hydrosol
- 1 teaspoon or 40 milliliters of alcohol (96 percent ABV)
- 2 drops of essential oil

Hair care

Shampoo
Like the shower gel, shampoo requires soft soap, which has active detergent properties. Again, you can get more lather by using more soft soap.

Heat the water or the hydrolate to about 140°F (60°C), dissolve the soft soap in it, and then add the alcohol. Once the mixture has cooled down to about 86°F (30°C), add the drops of essential oil.
Example: 25 drops of rosemary oil, balsam poplar hydrosol

You need:
- 3.4 fluid ounces (100 milliliters) of water or hydrosol
- 40 grams of soft soap
- 7 milliliters of alcohol (96 percent ABV)
- 25 drops of essential oil

Hair tonic (conditioner)
Dissolve the essential oil in alcohol and then mix it with water. If hydrosol is used instead of water, adding essential oil isn't absolutely necessary.
Example: 6 drops of lavender oil and/or rosemary hydrosol

You need:
- 3.4 fluid ounces (100 milliliters) of distilled water or hydrosol
- 1 teaspoon of alcohol (96 percent ABV)
- 6 drops of essential oil

Soap

Bring the water to a boil, add the carrier oil and the wax, wait until the wax is melted, and then slowly add the soap flakes while stirring. Once you've added half of the flakes, remove the beaker from the stove and stir in the rest—watch out, it will foam! Stir constantly until the mixture is lukewarm. Add the drops of essential oil and stir well again.

You can shape it using any sort of mold you want. There are no restrictions on your imagination: ice cube trays, empty coffee creamer or yogurt cups, baking pans, sand molds, etc. After a week,

You need:
- 50 grams of soap flakes or odorless grated soap
- 0.5 grams of beeswax
- 1.7 fluid ounces (50 milliliters) of water
- 5 milliliters of neutral carrier oil
- 3 drops of essential oil

remove the soap from the mold and let it dry at room temperature for a few weeks.

You can make multicolored soap by adding a few drops of food coloring (see also bath salts). Let the previous color dry before adding the next one over it. You can also place decorative items such as dried fruits, small figurines, small mussels, pearls, herbs, etc., between the layers. Very often lavender blossoms are added for use as an exfoliant.

Let the finished soap sit in the mold or in paper, and turn it over after two to three weeks. The soap should dry for a total of four to five months. According to one soap maker, a drop of alcohol makes the soap smoother and more pleasant. It's worth trying, at least.

Example: 5 milliliters of almond or thistle oil and 3 drops of juniper or lavender oil

Perfume

You need:
- 8 milliliters of jojoba oil
- 2 milliliters of essential oil
- 1 drop of thistle oil per 10 milliliters of perfume

or
- 8 milliliters of alcohol (96 percent ABV)
- 2 milliliters of essential oil
- 1 drop of thistle oil per 10 milliliters of perfume

Note: A perfume's fragrance is a combination of 50–150 different scents.

Perfumes have an essential oil content of 20 percent, meaning that 10 milliliters of perfume contains 2 milliliters of pure essential oil. They can be made from a single essential oil, but they're usually made of a mixture of more than one, in which case the perfume is made up of the following notes:

- *Overtone:* This is the first scent that is perceived. It's light and delicate. It's perceptible on the skin for between five minutes and two hours.
- *Heart:* The perfume's true fragrance, soft, aromatic, and flowery. It remains present for two to twelve hours.
- *Base note:* The earthy, balsamic, deep fragrance that lingers the longest, for twelve to twenty-four hours.

The overtone, heart, and base note structure was developed by Jean Carles in 1940 and remains the norm in perfume production to this day. Each individual note contains at least three different oils, meaning that the perfume has a total of at least nine different fragrances. Usually, however, they're made up of 50–150 different fragrant substances. The overtone and heart each contain a quarter of the total fragrant oil while the base note contains the other half. So if you want to produce 10 milliliters of perfume, you need a total of 2 milliliters of essential oil, of which 0.5 milliliters each is allotted to the overtone and heart and 1 milliliter to the base note.

If you want to produce a perfume professionally, you should blend the oils with alcohol before mixing them together, creating a 20 percent oil-alcohol mixture. For example, you could take 2 milliliters of juniper oil and fill it up to 10 milliliters with alcohol.

Soap production

▲ Boil the water, add first the wax and then the carrier oil.

▲ When the wax is melted, add the soap flakes carefully (watch for foaming!) while stirring continuously; remove the beaker glass from the hot plate when all the soap is added.

▲ Stir until the mixture is lukewarm, then add the drops of essential oil.

▲ Then pour the soap into small boxes or other molds.

If you mix the essential oils directly, it will be almost impossible to smell the composition's fragrance because the oils will be too highly concentrated.

The following overview shows you which plants are especially suitable for which notes:

Overtone, heart, and base note ▸

Oil type	Plant
Overtone	Anise, bay, bergamot, horseradish, lemon, lime, mustard, rosemary, tangerine, thyme, vervain
Overtone or heart	Angelica, basil, grapefruit, lemon balm, lemongrass, lily of the valley,* mountain pine, myrtle, orange blossoms, parsley, pepper, peppermint, petitgrain (lemon), pine
Heart	Caraway, cardamom, carrot, celery, cilantro, clove, cypress, davana, dill, eucalyptus, fennel, ginger, hyacinth, jasmine, juniper, lavender, lily, lovage, marigold, marjoram, mint, mugwort, nutmeg, rockrose, Roman chamomile, sage, savory, tarragon, thuja, turmeric, valerian
Heart or base note	Birch, cedar, cinnamon, clary sage, geranium, hops, hyssop, iris, magnolia, patchouli, petitgrain (orange, tangerine), rose, star anise, tuberose, violet, wattle, ylang-ylang
Base note	Arrufiac, bay leaf, benzoin, broom, frankincense, garlic, German chamomile, jasmine, musk,* myrrh, narcissus, oakmusk,* oregano, patchouli, sandalwood, vetiver, wattle, white musk*
* Artificial products widespread in the perfume industry	

Because the nose becomes "numb" fairly quickly when smelling many different fragrances, you should always consider the following when mixing perfumes:

1. Mix the base note first. Try to find three fragrances that have already been diluted with alcohol.
2. Dip a cardboard strip in each base note fragrance and label them.
3. Hold the strips in a fan shape and slowly fan them past your nose.
4. Are you satisfied with the overall fragrance, or does one component stand out especially? If so, switch out one of the cardboard strips and repeat the smell test.
5. After the base note, do the same thing for the heart. If you're happy with it as well, combine the heart with the base note and see how they are as a whole.
6. Repeat the process for the overtone.

Using Your Oils

◂ A perfumer, the "nose," composes fragrances on a so-called perfume organ.

7. As soon as you've found the composition you want, take 1 milliliter each of the alcoholic dilutions. Make sure to preserve the proper ratio between the three notes.

After you've gotten familiar with this process, you can also use somewhat less of the very strongly fragrant oils or more of the weaker fragrances or use different types of oil. Just be sure not to change the ratio between the overtone, heart, and base note.

After you've mixed the components together, you shouldn't shake the bottle; just tilt it back and forth a couple of times. Then the perfume needs at least one to three months in darkness to mature. Add thistle oil (1 drop per 10 milliliters of perfume), patchouli oil, or oakmoss oil to the perfume as a fixative so that the fragrances stay on your skin longer. If the perfume is cloudy after being stored, you can filter the cloudiness out with pre-folded paper filters (fluted filters) grade 1.

The following other fragrant products also exist in addition to perfume. They're differentiated from each other by their oil contents and by how perceptible they are on the skin.

Product	Oil content	Amount of time it lasts on the skin
Perfume	20%	One day
Eau de parfum	15%	Four to five hours
Eau de toilette	10%	Two hours
Eau de cologne	5%	Brief refresher

Example of lady's perfume:
- Overtone (0.5 milliliters): 0.1 milliliters of bergamot, 0.3 milliliters of lime, 0.1 milliliters of tangerine
- Heart (0.5 milliliters): 0.3 milliliters of rose, 0.1 milliliters of lavender, 0.1 milliliters of sage
- Base note (1 milliliter): 0.2 milliliters of bay leaf, 0.4 milliliters of oregano, 0.4 milliliters of geranium

Example of gentleman's perfume:
- Overtone (0.5 milliliters): 0.1 milliliters of bergamot, 0.3 milliliters of lime, 0.1 milliliters of rosemary
- Heart (0.5 milliliters): 0.3 milliliters of lavender, 0.1 milliliters of lemongrass, 0.1 milliliters of sage
- Base note (1 milliliter): 0.2 milliliters of vetiver, 0.5 milliliters of sandalwood, 0.3 milliliters of cedar

Paper strips for checking the fragrance composition ▶

It's very easy to check whether a product is actually a perfume or "really just" eau de toilette or something else. You can do so by placing a drop on the back of your hand and rubbing it in. If it's perfume, you'll be able to clearly perceive its oily consistency.

Whenever you use perfume, you should keep in mind that you won't be able to perceive it any more yourself after a while because your nose will have adjusted to its fragrance. The people around you still will, however, so only use perfume very sparingly. One drop on each of the following parts of the body is enough: the inside of the wrist, the crook of the arm, behind the ears, at the base of the neck under the chin, on the décolletage (for women), and possibly also on the backs of the knees. Perfumes made from essential oils naturally have the same effects as the oils they're made from.

Aluminum bottles for storing perfume ▼

You can use more of the other fragrant products depending on their oil contents. With eau de cologne, for example, it's a good idea to spray the various locations once or twice each with a spray bottle at a distance of a little under a foot (30 centimeters).

> ☺ Tip: Always store perfume under cool, dry, and dark conditions. You can store it in glass bottles (for one to two years), but aluminum bottles are better (five years).

Liqueurs

As already mentioned in chapter 2, many liqueurs are also made with the help of essential oils nowadays. You should use alcohol that is as tasteless as possible and, of course, not denatured (i.e., drinkable). It's best to use rectified spirit after diluting it to the desired alcohol content with demineralized (distilled) water. With a little bit of expertise, you can even make the alcohol yourself. Hydrosols are nothing but distilled water and soluble compounds of essential oils, so they can be used to dilute the alcohol as well. In all of the following recipes, you can substitute the essential oils for the hydrosols when the high-percentage rectified spirit is partially diluted with hydrosols instead of water. However, because homemade hydrosols can be extremely intense, you should use them diluted to a ratio of approximately 1:7 to 1:10. For the sugar, so-called inverted sugar syrup or liquid fructose is best. One quart (one liter) of inverted sugar syrup is equivalent to 2.2 pounds (1 kilogram) of "normal" granulated sugar. It has the advantages of not having to be tediously boiled, the sugar not returning to crystal form, and the drink's flavor standing out more due to less interference thanks to the inverted sugar's milder sweetness.

A liqueur should never be enjoyed fresh, but rather after being stored in glass bottles for a few months (never use plastic, and store it in the darkest possible conditions at room temperature) so that the scent and flavor have a chance to fully round out. You have the option of filtering it at this point. If you want to reduce the amount of time this rounding out takes, you can also use atmospheric oxygen to age the liqueur artificially by mixing it for about two to three minutes per quart (liter) while it foams (!) with an electric handheld blender, a milk frother, an electric cocktail mixer, or something similar. It doesn't matter what you use; what's important is to mix air into the liquid.

Absinthe flavor, Swiss style I
1.00 quart (0.95 liters) of 40 percent ABV alcohol
1.76 ounces (50 grams) of sugar
Wormwood oil, 0.4 milliliters
Anise oil, 0.1 milliliters
Cilantro oil, 0.2 milliliters

Absinthe flavor, Swiss style II
1.00 quart (0.95 liters) of 40 percent ABV alcohol
1.76 ounces (50 grams) of sugar
Wormwood oil, 0.5 milliliters
Orange oil, 0.2 milliliters
Star anise oil, 0.1 milliliters
Orange blossom oil, 0.05 milliliters
Lemon oil, 0.1 milliliters

Anise I
1.00 quart (0.95 liters) of
  40 percent ABV alcohol
1.76 ounces (50 grams) of sugar
0.4 milliliters of anise oil

Anise II
1.00 quart (0.95 liters) of
  40 percent ABV alcohol
1.76 ounces (50 grams) of sugar
0.25 milliliters of anise oil
0.15 milliliters of fennel oil

Caraway
1.03 quarts (0.975 liters) of
  40 percent ABV alcohol
0.88 ounces (25 grams) of sugar
Caraway oil, 0.4 milliliters

Caraway, Breslau style
0.90 quarts (0.85 liters) of
  40 percent ABV alcohol
5.29 ounces (150 grams)
  of sugar
Caraway oil, 0.6 milliliters
Fennel oil, 5 drops
Cilantro oil, 10 drops
Anise oil, 8 drops

Caraway, Danzig style
1.00 quart (0.95 liters) of
  40 percent ABV alcohol
1.76 ounces (50 grams) of sugar
Caraway oil, 0.5 milliliters
Orange oil, 3 drops
Cilantro oil, 5 drops

Carmelite style
1.00 quart (0.95 liters) of
  40 percent ABV alcohol
1.76 ounces (50 grams) of sugar
Orange peel oil, 0.3 milliliters
Cilantro oil, 0.1 milliliters
Lemon balm oil, 0.1 milliliters
Lemon oil, 0.05 milliliters

Cherry
0.95 quarts (0.90 liters) of
  40 percent ABV alcohol
100 milliliters of cherry syrup
Lemon oil, 5 drops
Clove oil, 5 drops

Jenever style
1.00 quart (0.95 liters) of
  40 percent ABV alcohol
1.76 ounces (50 grams) of sugar
0.6 milliliters of juniper oil

Krambambula
1.00 quart (0.95 liters) of
  40 percent ABV alcohol
1.76 ounces (50 grams) of sugar
Anise oil, 3 drops
Caraway oil, 2 drops
Lavender oil, 3 drops
Cardamom oil, 2 drops
Cinnamon oil, 5 drops
Clove oil, 3 drops
Lemon oil, 5 drops

Lemon
1.00 quart (0.95 liters) of
  40 percent ABV alcohol
1.76 ounces (50 grams) of sugar
Lemon oil, 0.4 milliliters
Orange oil, 0.05 milliliters
Cinnamon oil, 5 drops

Peppermint
1.00 quart (0.95 liters) of
  40 percent ABV alcohol
1.76 ounces (50 grams) of sugar
Peppermint oil, 0.4 milliliters

Using Your Oils

The following recipes are often also described as crèmes because of their thick consistencies due to their very high sugar contents. To ensure that the essential oils fully dissolve, you should mix them with the high-percentage alcohol first and then add the sugar and the water. You can also heat the mixture to about 104°F (40°C) so that the sugar dissolves better.

Anise
13.5 fluid ounces (0.4 liters) of 90 percent ABV alcohol
10.6 ounces (300 grams) of sugar
Water: fill to 1.1 quarts (1 liter)
Anise oil, 0.4 milliliters

Anisette
13.5 fluid ounces (0.4 liters) of 90 percent ABV alcohol
10.6 ounces (300 grams) of sugar
Water: fill to 1.1 quarts (1 liter)
Anise oil, 0.2 milliliters
Fennel oil, 0.05 milliliters
Star anise oil, 0.6 milliliters
Cilantro oil, 2 drops

Bitter liqueur
13.5 fluid ounces (0.4 liters) of 90 percent ABV alcohol
10.6 ounces (300 grams) of sugar
Water: fill to 1.1 quarts (1 liter)
Orange oil, 0.05 milliliters
Peppermint oil, 0.05 milliliters
Juniper oil, 0.1 milliliters
Anise oil, 0.05 milliliters
Clove oil, 0.05 milliliters
Wormwood oil, 0.05 milliliters
Lemon oil, 0.05 milliliters
Fennel oil, 0.05 milliliters

Caraway liqueur, Magdeburg style
13.5 fluid ounces (0.4 liters) of 90 percent ABV alcohol
10.6 ounces (300 grams) of sugar
Water: fill to 1.1 quarts (1 liter)
Caraway oil, 0.6 milliliters
Fennel oil, 2 drops
Anise oil, 0.05 milliliters
Lemon oil, 2 drops

Danziger Goldwasser style*
13.5 fluid ounces (0.4 liters) of 90 percent ABV alcohol
10.6 ounces (300 grams) of sugar
Water: fill to 1.1 quart (1 liter)
Lemon oil, 0.4 milliliters
Cilantro oil, 10 drops
Neroli oil, 6 drops
Orange oil, 6 drops
plus some flakes of real gold foil

---

* A German liqueur dating from 1598, known for the small flakes of gold suspended in the liqueur. This is not the exact recipe but should yield similar results.

Eisenbahn (railroad) liqueur*
13.5 fluid ounces (0.4 liters) of 90 percent ABV alcohol
10.6 ounces (300 grams) of sugar
Water: fill to 1.1 quarts (1 liter)
Cinnamon oil, 0.2 milliliters
Clove oil, 0.1 milliliters
Anise oil, 10 drops
Peppermint oil, 0.2 milliliters
Rose oil, 2 drops

Peppermint liqueur I
13.5 fluid ounces (0.4 liters) of 90 percent ABV alcohol
10.6 ounces (300 grams) of sugar
Water: fill to 1.1 quarts (1 liter)
Peppermint oil, 0.4 milliliters

Peppermint liqueur II
13.5 fluid ounces (0.4 liters) of 90 percent ABV alcohol
10.6 ounces (300 grams) of sugar
Water: fill to 1.1 quarts (1 liter)
Peppermint oil, 0.45 milliliters
Lemon oil, 0.05 milliliters

Raspberry
13.5 fluid ounces (0.4 liters) of 90 percent ABV alcohol
16.9 fluid ounces (500 milliliters) of raspberry syrup
Water: fill to 1.1 quarts (1 liter)
Citric acid, 1.0 gram
Orange flower water, 25 milliliters

Rose liqueur
13.5 fluid ounces (0.4 liters) of 90 percent ABV alcohol
10.6 ounces (300 grams) of sugar
Water: fill to 1.1 quarts (1 liter)
Rose oil, 0.1 milliliters
Orange flower water, 25 milliliters

*Presumably a well-known liqueur around the time of the nineteenth century. The recipes for this and the other liqueurs in this chapter were found in an old German pharmacy book printed around the 1920s.

Miscellaneous

As already mentioned, uses for essential oils and hydrosols aren't confined to cosmetics and liqueurs. They can also be used in cooking, such as for **flavoring food**, **spiced oils**, **salads**, or **drinks**. When you're working with food, it's especially important for your oils to be pure and not fake (see page 14).

The newest trend in gourmet cooking is **spiced oils**, fine cooking oils enriched with essential oils. They're usually sprayed on salads or similar dishes with a spray bottle shortly before serving. The following oil mixtures are just given as examples—you can of course alter them to taste or come up with your own creations: 3.4 ounces (100 milliliters) of olive oil with 4 drops of marjoram oil, 3 drops of lovage oil, 2 drops of dill oil, 2 drops of fennel oil and 2 drops of pepper oil (black or green). Lemon or orange oil are especially good for seasoning desserts and baked goods.

Hydrosols are very well-suited for soft drinks. For example, a lemon hydrosol mixed with sparkling mineral water at a ratio of approximately 1:10 or even less is very refreshing. Other examples include orange, lime, lemongrass, or lemon verbena. Rose, lavender, marigold, and geranium are the best bases for a glamorous floral drink to be served on special (romantic) occasions. And don't forget cocktails! A restaurateur recently told me that she'd begun to offer a mixture of prune plum brandy and lavender hydrosol to her patrons. It wasn't long before this drink became the hit of the year.

You can even flavor **black tea** with essential oils. Either add one drop to the tea leaves before you brew the tea or add about 5 drops of oil per 3.5 ounces (100 grams) of tea. Earl Grey tea consists of a mixture of black tea and bergamot oil. Shake well in a closed container, and store.

For **sauna infusions**, you should add 5–20 drops of essential oil, depending on the type and the desired intensity, per quart (liter) of water. About 2–5 drops per ladleful is enough. Hydrosols of the "typical" sauna oils (mountain pine and other conifers, mint, citrus, lemongrass, etc.) can be used pure rather than in the typical oil-water-mixture. In most cases one ladleful is sufficient.

For **fragrant oil burners**, use some water and 3–10 drops of essential oil. Don't let the liquids dry up, or the lamp will be left with a brown, resinous residue that can only be removed with acetone or nail polish remover. Or, as with the sauna infusion, fill the burner with pure, undiluted hydrosols. For this method, learn to trust your nose. After about two-thirds to three-quarters (depending on the type) of the added amount has evaporated, you will recognize an unpleasant smell, the result of the hydrosol overheating. This scent indicates that it's time to empty the burner, wash it, and use a fresh portion of hydrosol.

The most important essential oils for cooking are: Anise oil, tarragon oil, cilantro oil, caraway oil, lavender oil, nutmeg oil, oregano oil, peppermint oil, rose oil, cinnamon oil, lemon oil.

Potpourri can be aromatized with essential oils or hydrosols, allowing them to function as air fresheners. Who doesn't appreciate a pleasant scent in the bathroom, for example?

For **air freshener sprays**, add essential oil or a hydrosol to 96 percent ABV alcohol (about 20 drops of oil per quart [liter]), or 8.5 fluid ounces (250 milliliters) of hydrosol.

You can use hydrosols directly on **gauze pads**. Alternatively, you can add 3 milliliters of essential oil to 1 quart (1 liter) of water and soak the pads in it.

Add 2–6 drops of essential oil to a bowl containing 1 pint (0.5 liters) of hot water to create an **inhalant**, or use a hydrosol that has been diluted at a ratio of about 1:4, depending on the type.

You can **clean** the floors, cupboards, etc. in your home with a few drops of essential oil in mopping water. It smells pleasant and has a minor disinfecting effect. In principle, you don't need to add any other cleaning material. Hydrosols are similarly effective.

You can make fragrant **ironing water** by adding about 2–3 drops of essential oil to distilled water or using the hydrosol directly. If the hydrosol's fragrance is too intense, you can dilute it with distilled water at a 1:1 ratio or shake it to lower the essential oil content (see page 100).

If you dry your **laundry** in your living space, you can give the area a nice scent by adding a few drops of essential oil into the washing machine during the last rinse cycle. This is how we use our old leftover oils.

> ☺ Tip: Don't add citrus or mint oils to your washing machine as they can attack its plastic parts.

CHAPTER 6

Frequently Asked Questions

Since theory and practice famously don't always agree, we're including the following examples of typical questions that have come up in the (German) discussion corner on our website. You can find the complete and current version at www.aetherischesoel.at. Our English online services can be found at the end of the book.

Lemon balm

Can I extract oil from regular lemon balm from my garden? Could you theoretically also add drops of lemon balm oil to juices, alcohol, etc., as a sort of substitute for artificial essences? If so, could you cook with it, too?

Of course you can use regular lemon balm from your garden. Incidentally, lemon balm oil is one of the most expensive oils in the world, and it doesn't produce particularly high yields. A couple of drops of oil is plenty, though. You can add drops of the oil to juices, alcohol, etc., and cook with it. But be careful with the dosage and keep in mind that essential oils can sometimes be toxic at high concentrations, so you should always be careful when ingesting it (see page 119). You shouldn't forget the valuable hydrosol. It can be used as an alternative for or in addition to the essential oil.

Rectified spirit instead of alcohol

I have a question about making perfume. Is it true that the main component is alcohol? Can I use rectified spirit from a pharmacy? As far as I know, special denatured alcohol is always used in perfumes, similar to the spirit that so many people have allergic reactions to.

That is correct. Denatured alcohol is used in making perfume. However, it's mixed with a different substance than methylated spirit so that it doesn't irritate skin. It is possible to have an allergic reaction to the additives that are in it, though. You can also use rectified spirit, or ethanol, in place of denatured alcohol in perfume production.

Dried herbs

Is it possible to make essential oil from dried herbs?

I recently worked with dried peppermint—the cheap peppermint leaves that are sold in large quantities for tea at supermarkets, in fact. It was hard to believe how much oil came out of them.

Hydrosol

I leave the little bottles with the hydrosol and the yellow sage oil above it sitting for three to four weeks to let the cloudiness settle out. Can I increase my oil yield by leaving the bottles in the freezer during this period? Wouldn't the oil have to come out of the hydrosol better?

Your point about freezing is correct in theory, but in practice it won't bring you any benefit. Let the bottles sit for three to four weeks like you're already doing anyway and then remove the essential oil. The next time you distill sage, you can use the hydrosol in the still instead of fresh water. This will allow you to produce more oil because the water is already saturated with it.

Cleaning the still

Can I also make my own essential oils with my schnapps still (stainless steel pot and glass condenser)? Surely the still will be kind of "oily" after distilling oil with it? How can I clean it afterward?

There's no reason why not. What you will definitely need, however, is a steamer basket, so that the herbs are steamed and not cooked. Furthermore, the steam chamber should have a large enough capacity that enough oil comes out during distillation. To clean the still: first, rinse it out thoroughly with not-denatured, rectified spirit, then with water and dish soap.

Medical treatment

Can homemade essential oils such as those made with a Leonardo still also be used for medicinal purposes? Can they be mixed into a massage oil or body oil? I assume that they can definitely be used with fragrant oil burners at any rate.

Of course you can also use the oils for medicinal purposes. It just depends on the initial materials you used. If the herbs were treated with certain sprays, for example, I wouldn't use the oils because the toxins can be brought along during the distillation, too. You should therefore only use organic herbs. I recommend caution if ingesting pure, undiluted essential oils. Some oils are highly toxic at these concentrations. You should always consult with a doctor before doing so. For body and massage oils, you just need to add a couple of drops of pure essential oil to a so-called carrier oil (odorless oils such as jojoba oil), or you can even mix multiple essential oils together. The oils can also be used with fragrant oil burners (see page 119).

Leonardo or Deluxe?

Which still is better for producing essential oils, the Leonardo or the Deluxe?

Which still is better depends on what you want to distill and how you're planning to use it. For herbs that contain a small amount of oil, the Leonardo is better because almost no oil gets stuck in its cooling system thanks to the very short length and the special shape of its condenser. With this still you can obtain the largest possible yield of essential oils per pound (kilogram) plant material (see page 33). Furthermore, all inner parts can be cleaned thoroughly by hand with dishwashing liquid and a cleaning sponge scourer. But it's not reasonable possible to distill alcohol with the Leonardo. The Deluxe, on the other hand, is an alcohol still that can also be used to produce essential oils and hydrosols. The disadvantage: a small amount of essential oil remains in the condenser. Therefore after distilling, the condenser worm has to be rinsed out with rectified spirit (afterwards the spirit can be used as perfume) to avoid spoiling the distillate of the next run.

Small stills

A steam generator is always used when essential oils are produced professionally via steam distillation. If you only have a small still, can you still expect a high-quality product?

Yes. Small stills include a steamer basket that allows the material you're distilling (e.g., roses) to be inside the steam chamber and for the steam to carry the oil along with it. This is what makes it possible to produce high-quality essential oil with a small still as well. Stills in which the material being distilled is in the boiling water are not really suitable for making aromatic oils.

Mixing oils

I know that if I use multiple different raw materials (e.g., sage from Italy and sage from Germany), the quality of the oil can vary and that the quality of mixtures is also different. But how big is the difference in quality if the distilling just took place at different times? From an economic standpoint, it would be very costly to store every two drops separately if you're extracting two drops of oil at a time.

If you've distilled the same kind of plant more than once, it's fine to mix the oil together. For the sake of completeness, however, I should mention that the quality of the essential oil varies during the distillation process. The best and most valuable oil comes first. The longer the distillation goes on, the lower the quality becomes. This isn't really relevant for home distillers, but expensive oils such as ylang-ylang are sold in different fractions at different prices.

Oil receiver container

What can I do if the essential oil has collected on the receiver container (glass) in the form of little droplets?

Quickly spinning the bottle vertically can shake the oil together somewhat. If it's spread very thin, however, that won't do any good. Be sure to use an oil receiver container that becomes very narrow at the top. This will keep you from encountering this problem again in the future. For now, all you can do is to try to consolidate the oil with a glass rod to form larger droplets. Or you can use this product the next time you distill instead of adding water and the oil will come out again along with the new oil.

Green rust (verdigris)

I haven't used my still in a long time and green rust (verdigris) has unfortunately formed on the condenser. What should I do so that I can use it again? How can I keep this from happening in the future?

Place the condenser in a very hot citric acid bath with about 3.5 ounces (100 grams) of citric acid per quart (liter) of water for about an hour and then clean it very thoroughly with water and dish soap. Then rinse it out intensely with hot water. You can avoid green rust by always leaving the still open when you store it and never storing it in humid locations.

Alcohol production

I've been distilling my own essential oils and making my own perfumes for a while. Would it be possible to start making the alcohol for the perfume myself too? Rectified spirit from the pharmacy is pretty expensive, after all. Is there an easy way to do this?

Of course you can make tasteless alcohol yourself. One simple method is alcoholic-sugar fermentation. You can find more information in our book *The Artisan's Guide to Crafting Distilled Spirits*, published in English by Acres U.S.A.

Solvents

Is it possible to use liquids other than water when making essential oils? I can imagine that you might be able to attain a higher oil yield by using alcohol because essential oils are more soluble in alcohol than in water.

It's true that essential oils are more soluble in alcohol. If you distilled eucalyptus with alcohol, for example, the result would be a wonderful eucalyptus spirit with a couple of drops of oil at most floating on the top. But precisely because the oil is more soluble, there's no way to separate it any more. You'd have to evaporate all of the alcohol and then use the residue. I would advise against trying this method at home because the repeated heating would destroy more of the aroma than you would get at the end. In commercial operations, an organic solvent (e.g., hexane) is usually used in place of water, which significantly improves yields. However, the solvent has to be evaporated afterward, and some remnants are always left behind in the oil. The idea of putting these solvents on your skin in the form of a cream, for example, is somewhat alarming. If you make the oil yourself, be sure just to use water so that it's free of chemicals.

Lavender

Somehow, my attempts to produce essential oils aren't working out quite right. Last time, I distilled about 500 grams of lavender in 4 liters of water. The distillate smelled a little like lavender, but I didn't produce any oil. Where could I have gone wrong?

You don't need any more than 1 liter of water in the kettle for 500 grams of lavender. The distillation will be over by the time about 400 milliliters of water has been distilled. Did you boil the lavender in the water? You should definitely not do that. Herbs should always be in the steam chamber. It's also important to cut up the plants well beforehand; not doing so will lower your oil yield considerably. Furthermore, your yield obviously also depends on the type of lavender. Spike lavender produces minimal oil, while lavandin produces a considerable amount. And finally, the type of still you use is crucial to how much oil you get: a former schnapps distiller managed to receive no oil at all from his professional 20-gallon (75-liter) column still for alcohol. The column withheld the entire oil. Stills with a Leonardo-style condenser should produce significantly more oil than stills with a worm because a certain amount of the oil becomes stuck in the worm during cooling. But we were contacted by a small commercial distiller with such a still who received no oil because the connection between kettle and condenser was far too narrow (see page 28).

High altitudes

I'm interested in cultivating aromatic plants and distilling them in large amounts. Can the plants be cultivated at an elevation of 700 meters? In our area, large amounts of juniper are accrued when the juniper heath is pruned. Would they be worth distilling?

An elevation 700 meters above sea level is no problem. For example, the classic lavender of Provence is cultivated at an elevation of nearly 2,000 feet (600 meters) above sea level. What's important is that the plants produce enough oil, which means they need lots of sun. You can make excellent oil from juniper berries, but you can also use the needles and twigs (see page 79). You can get a very large amount of oil from crushed dried berries.

Distilling or cold pressing?

What's the difference between oils that were produced via distillation and oils that were produced via cold pressing?

Only a few essential oils can be cold pressed. Oranges, tangerines, limes, and lemons are suitable for producing essential oils via this method. All other essential oils can only be extracted via steam distillation or solvent extraction. With citrus fruits, the oils obtained from distillation should be clear, colorless liquids with a fine scent, whereas the pressed oils will be colored and cloudy because they contain lots of waxes and resins. Non-essential, fatty oils—such as corn oil, pumpkin seed oil, olive oil, etc.—are also cold pressed, even from sprouts, seeds, etc.

Undiluted oil can be dangerous!

I distilled some peppermint, producing a very good yield. I accidentally let a couple of drops of oil fall onto the tablecloth (composite material: fabric with thin foamy plastic over it). The essential oil ate a hole in it! Is the oil dangerous?

Most essential oils are very aggressive (e.g., will attack polystyrene), and some are also toxic. They're highly concentrated and should therefore not be used without medical knowledge, and only in their diluted forms. However, rubbing a drop of oil into the back of your hand to test its fragrance is completely safe.

Afterword

Every two months, we host seminars on fragrant oils in which each participant produces two different essential oils and hydrosols using stills that we provide. Participants then separate the oil from the hydrosol and use it to create soaps, perfumes, massage oils, and bath salts. All self-produced products can be taken home.

Although the main language used during the workshops is German, it is possible for English-speaking participants to follow the context due to the course structure.

Apart from that, it is possible for us to instruct single persons or small groups in English at any time; contact us for more information.

Are you interested but unable to visit us or to combine your trip with a holiday in beautiful Carinthia? Then attend our online seminars at www.distilling-fermenting-seminars.com!

Our stills and all other necessary equipment described in this book are available for order worldwide via www.aetherischesoel.at.

Contact address:
Dr. Bettina Malle und Dr. Helge Schmickl
Ehrentalerstr. 39
9020 Klagenfurt
Austria / European Union

Tel./Fax: 0043-(0)463-437786
E-mail: schmickl@aetherischesoel.at
Homepage: www.aetherischesoel.at

◀ One of Malle and Schmickl's fragrant oil seminars

▲ A seminar participant's finished products (example):
- About 17 U.S. fluid ounces (500 milliliters) of lavender hydrosol
- About 17 U.S. fluid ounces (500 milliliters) of clove hydrosol
- 12 milliliters of lavender oil (amount depends on the type of plant used)
- 11 milliliters of clove oil (amount depends on the type of plant used)
- 5 milliliters of perfume with essential oils
- 10 milliliters of massage oil with essential oils
- 3.5 ounces (100 grams) of fragrant soap with essential oils
- 1.8 ounces (50 grams) of bath salts with essential oils

Since not all participants will distill the same plants, you may also use essential oils other than the ones you make yourself in your cosmetic products.

Harvest Calendar

The following calendar is suitable for European and North American continental climate and the adjacent regions of surrounding climatic zones.

	Jan.	Feb.	Mar.	Apr.	May	Jun.	Jul.	Aug.	Sep.	Oct.	Nov.	Dec.
Angelica									■	■		
Anise							■	■	■			
Basil						■	■	■	■			
Bay leaf						■	■	■	■			
Birch				■	■							
Caraway							■	■				
Carrot								■	■	■		
Cedar					■	■	■	■	■	■		
Celery								■	■	■		
Chamomile						■	■	■				
Cilantro							■	■	■			
Clary sage							■	■				
Cotton lavender							■	■				
Cypress						■						
Dill							■	■				
Elecampane									■	■		
Fennel							■	■	■			
Garlic							■	■				
Geranium							■	■	■			
Ground ivy					■							
Hogweed							■	■				
Hops								■	■			
Hyssop							■	■				
Jasmine							■	■	■			
Juniper			■	■								
Larch						■	■	■				
Lavender							■	■				
Lemon balm						■	■	■	■			

Harvest Calendar

	Jan	Feb	Mar	Apr	May	Jun	Jul	Aug	Sep	Oct	Nov	Dec
Lemon verbena						■	■	■				
Lovage						■	■	■				
Marigold						■	■	■				
Marjoram						■	■	■				
Mint						■	■	■				
Mountain pine					■	■	■	■				
Mugwort							■	■				
Myrtle						■	■	■				
Oakmoss		■	■									
Oregano						■	■	■				
Parsley						■	■	■				
Pine					■	■	■	■				
Ramson				■								
Rose						■	■					
Rosemary					■	■	■	■				
Sage						■	■	■				
Savory						■	■	■				
Signet marigold						■	■					
Spruce					■	■	■	■				
St. John's wort						■	■	■				
Strawflower						■	■	■				
Tarragon						■	■	■				
Thuja					■	■	■	■	■	■		
Thyme						■	■	■				
Valerian									■	■		
Violet				■	■							
Wormwood						■	■	■				
Yarrow						■	■	■				

Index

absinthe, 91, 115
acetone, 27–28, 42–43, 119
acne, 93
air freshener, 92, 120
alcohol, 5, 6, 12, 14, 19, 27–28, 34
alcohol production
allspice, 66
almond oil, 8, 54, 97
aluminum, 26, 57, 114
angelica, 66, 98, 101, 112
anise, 43, 61, 65, 66, 93, 101, 112, 116, 117, 119
anti-foam, 46, 76, 77
anxiety, 77, 86, 91, 93
aromatherapy, 3, 6, 10, 14, 15, 33, 91, 92, 144
automatic oil separator, 51,
Avicenna, 2
avocado oil, 8, 98

bark, 1, 5, 11, 40, 42, 47, 69, 72
base note, 77, 110, 112–13
basil, 68, 101, 112
bath salts, 102, 131

bay laurel, 68
bay leaves, 39, 42, 61, 65, 93, 101, 112
bay rum tree, 68
beaker, 100, 111
beeswax, 99, 103–9
benzoin, 68, 112
bergamot, 11, 54, 69, 98, 112, 119
birch, 69, 93, 98, 112
bitter orange, 69, 98
blood pressure, 72, 76, 78, 80, 86, 87, 93, 94, 101
branches, 38, 41, 42, 67, 69, 72
bronchitis, 67, 77, 81, 87, 93
broom, 69, 112

cajuput, 70, 98, 101
camphor, 7, 10, 70, 93, 101
cananga. *See* ylang-ylang
caraway, 8, 39, 42, 43, 65, 70, 101, 112, 116, 117, 119
carbon dioxide extraction, 14

Index

cardamom, 70, 101, 112
carrier oil, 14, 56, 89, 97, 99, 100, 103–9, 124
carrot, 85, 112
cedar, 1, 5, 11, 61, 71, 98, 112
celery, 71, 112
cellulite, 93
chamomile, 11, 71–72, 93–94, 112
champaca, 92
chemotype, 7
cinnamon, 1, 43, 65, 72, 101, 112
  bark, 5, 40, 42, 72
citronella, 68, 72, 98
citrus, 11, 19, 37–39, 42, 43, 46, 54, 61, 80, 101, 120, 127
clary sage, 72, 101, 112
cleaning the plant, 19, 42, 54
cleaning the equipment, 27–28, 32, 33, 42–43, 47, 49, 52, 124–25
cleaning with essential oils, 1, 120
clementine, 73
clove, 65, 73, 93, 101, 112
coconut oil, 57, 108
co-distillation. *See under* distillation
cold pressing, 11, 54–56, 80, 127
compressing, 43, 46
concrete, 12, 13, 91
cooler, 28
corn oil, 54, 98, 127
cutter mixer, 39–40, 80
cypress, 74, 93, 98, 99, 101, 112

davana, 74, 112
Deluxe still, 34–35, 124–25
deodorant, 1, 81, 84, 87, 88, 108
depression, 69, 93
diarrhea, 93
digestive problems, 93
dill, 74, 112, 119
distillation
  co-distillation, 11
  double, 47–48
  fractional, 10, 47, 76, 92
  steam, 6, 9–10, 11, 12, 14, 19–35, 53, 125, 127
dome condenser, 2, 31, 32, 65
Douglas fir, 76
dried plants, 1, 36, 37, 38, 39, 40, 42, 53, 65–66, 123, 127

elecampane, 74
emulsifier, 100, 101, 105
enfleurage, 13–14, 56, 57–58, 69, 78, 83, 89, 91, 92
epilepsy, 101
essence, 1, 2, 7, 8, 123
essencier, 52
eucalyptus, 5, 7, 65, 74–75, 93–94, 98, 99, 101, 112
extraction method, 11–14

facial and body care, 98, 103–14
fake oils, 3, 5, 7, 14–16, 71, 84, 119
fatigue, 86, 93
fennel, 38, 61, 65, 75, 93–94, 98, 101, 112

fermentation, 38, 86, 126
fixative, 68, 72, 91, 113
Florentine flask. *See* essencier
food processor, 38–40, 42, 80
footbath, 98, 103
fragrant oil burner, 8, 16, 93, 98, 119, 124

garden shredder, 41, 42
garlic, 76, 112
gas chromatography, 14–15
geranium, 10, 15–16, 76–77, 93–94, 98, 100, 112, 119
ginger, 5, 8, 70, 77, 93–94, 98, 101, 112
grapefruit, 54, 77, 98, 112
ground ivy, 77

hair care, 8, 98, 109
hair loss, 68, 93
harvest, 35–38, 65
headaches, 67, 78, 82, 87, 89, 91, 93
heart note, 110, 112–13
hemp, 77
hogweed, 78
honey, 6, 102–4, 109
hops, 78, 112
hot plate, 45, 111
hyacinth, 89, 112
hydrosol, 5–6, 9, 20, 23, 24, 31, 33, 45, 47–52, 62, 99, 100, 115, 119, 123, 124
hyssop, 78, 94, 101, 112

incense, 1, 68–69, 74, 84
industrial production, 12, 47, 52, 69

infusion, 14, 56
insect bites, 93
iris, 78, 112

jasmine, 5, 13, 36, 57, 78, 93–94, 98, 101, 112
jojoba oil, 8, 98
Joy, 92
juniper, 71, 79, 93–94, 98, 101, 112, 127
  juniper berry, 40, 42, 65, 127

kettle, 10, 21, 24, 25, 26, 27, 28, 29, 30–31, 33, 39, 43, 46, 51, 127
  tea kettle, 22–23

lanolin, 100, 103–6
larch, 79
lard, 13, 14, 57
laundry, 120
lavandin, 79–80, 101, 102, 127
lavender, 3, 5, 10, 15, 36, 65, 79–80, 93–94, 98, 110, 112, 119, 126–27
  cotton lavender, 73
  spike lavender, 7, 88
lemon, 5, 43, 46, 53, 54–55, 66, 80, 93, 98, 112, 116, 119, 127
lemon balm, 11, 67, 93–94, 98, 99, 101, 112, 123
lemon verbena, 80, 119
lemongrass, 11, 15, 80, 101, 112, 119
Leonardo stills, 31–34, 42, 65, 67, 124–25
Liebig condenser, 27
lily of the valley, 7, 112

Index

lime, 81, 112, 119, 127
liqueur, 9, 115–18
lotion, 8, 98
lovage, 81, 112, 119
lyne arm, 21–22, 26, 27, 34

macadamia oil, 8, 99
maceration, 14, 56–57
magnolia, 92, 98, 112
marigold, 21, 81, 98, 103, 112, 119
marjoram, 8, 81, 93–94, 101, 112, 119
massage oil, 1, 8, 11, 54, 81, 92, 93, 97, 98, 100, 108, 124
medicinal clay, 104
melissa. *See* lemon balm
menstrual issues, 94
milk, 6, 101–4
mimosa, 91
mint, 66, 82, 93, 98, 99, 101, 112, 119, 120
mortar and pestle, 39, 40, 42, 66, 70, 71, 72, 75, 85
mountain pine, 16, 38, 83, 98, 112, 119
mouthwash, 108
mugwort. *See* wormwood
myrrh, 1, 5, 83, 93, 101, 112
myrtle, 70, 83, 93, 98, 99, 112

narcissus, 83, 112
neroli, 16, 69, 83–84, 101
nervousness, 94
nutmeg, 83, 101, 112

oakmoss, 83, 113
oatmeal, 104

oil yield, 6, 28, 30, 31, 35, 37–38, 39, 41, 43, 54, 67, 71, 85, 87, 124, 126–27
olive oil, 54, 56, 99, 108, 119, 127
orange, 5, 39, 53, 54, 66, 83–84, 93, 98, 119, 127
orange blossom, 11, 99, 112
oregano, 8, 66, 84, 93, 101, 112

palmarosa, 84
palo santo, 84
Paracelsus, 2
paraffin oil, 16
parsley, 84, 112
Pasteur pipette, 49–50, 100–101
patchouli, 84, 98, 112, 113
pepper, 85, 101, 112, 119
peppermint, 39, 66, 82, 93–94, 98, 99, 112, 116, 118, 123, 128
perfume, 1, 2, 7, 9, 16, 54, 57, 68, 72, 81, 84, 86, 90, 91, 92, 98, 99, 110–14, 123, 126
petitgrain, 69, 83, 98, 112
pregnancy, 101
pressure cooker, 22, 23–24, 26, 28

Queen Anne's lace. *See* carrot

ramson, 85
receiver container, 10, 22, 26, 29, 42, 44, 45, 47, 68, 72, 84, 125

rectified spirit, 57, 99, 115, 123, 124–24, 126
resin, 1, 5, 11, 14, 47, 67–68, 76, 82, 83, 119, 127
rheumatism, 66, 68, 72, 80, 81, 83, 88, 89 94
rockrose, 85, 99, 101, 112
root, 5, 47, 66, 70, 73, 77, 78, 81, 84, 89, 90, 91, 101
rose, 61, 93–94, 98, 99, 112, 118, 119
    Damascus rose, 85–86
    rose geranium, 15–16, 76, 100
    rose oil production, 5, 10, 13, 35, 36, 47–48, 57, 85–86
    rose petals, 41, 42, 47
    rosewater, 47, 85
rosemary, 1, 5, 11, 43, 66, 86, 93–94, 98, 99, 101, 112
rosewood, 86

safety precautions, 101, 128
sage, 5, 87, 93–94, 98, 99, 101, 112, 124
salt, 47, 48, 57, 102, 104
sandalwood, 1, 5, 81, 87, 98, 99, 112
sauna infusion, 98, 119
savory, 87, 101, 112
scale, 100
Scotch pine, 87
seeds, 38, 39, 40, 42, 43, 47, 53, 127
sensitive skin, 101,
sesame oil, 99, 108
shea butter, 57
skin care, 8

sleep disorders, 94
soap
    dish soap, 43, 54, 80, 124, 126
    flakes, 97, 100
    production, 12, 16, 54, 57, 91, 92, 98, 109–11
    soft soap, 100, 103, 109
solvents, 6, 14, 126
    extraction, 12–13, 56, 68, 69, 76, 77, 78, 83, 89, 91, 127
spagyric, 7
spatula, 57, 58, 100
spearmint, 82
spikenard, 90
spruce, 33, 38, 42, 88, 94, 98
St. John's wort, 88, 98
star anise. *See* anise
steam distillation. *See under* distillation
steam generator, 29, 30, 125
steamer basket, 21, 23–24, 25, 26, 29, 30, 31, 43, 44, 47, 71, 125
still head, 21
stomach issues, 94
storage
    of distillate, 48
    of equipment, 24, 126
    of essential oils, 61–62, 125
    of perfumes, 3, 113, 114
    of plant material, 35–37, 38, 86
strawflower, 88
stress, 94
sunflower oil, 99
sunscreen, 108
syringe, 48–49, 52, 100–101

Index

tallow, 57
tangerine, 54, 69, 88, 112, 127
tansy, 88
tap water, 43–44
tea kettle, 22–23, 29
tea tree, 89, 93–94, 98, 99
thuja, 71, 89, 112
thyme, 1, 7, 61, 89, 93–94, 98, 99, 101, 112
Tiger Balm, 82
tuberose, 89, 112
turmeric, 89, 112

valerian, 5, 90, 112
verbena. *See* lemon verbena
verdigris, 31, 126
vetiver, 91, 112
vinegar, 20, 103
violet, 57, 91, 98, 112

walnut oil, 99
water-oil mixture, 22, 50, 100
wheat bran, 104
wheat germ oil, 8, 99, 108
wok, 22, 25–26
worm, 21, 26–28, 34, 125, 127
wormwood, 98, 112

yarrow, 91–92, 98
yellow jade orchid, 92
yield calculations, 48, 53–54, 65–66, 124–25
ylang-ylang, 47, 92–93, 98, 112, 125
yolk, 104

About the Authors

Bettina Malle and **Helge Schmickl** graduated from the Vienna University of Technology in 1991 with masters of science in chemical engineering and received doctorates in technical sciences in 1993. Each earned a bachelor of business administration degree from the Graduate School of Business Administration Zurich while designing, engineering, and commissioning industrial plants and managing research and development projects. Thereafter they worked as technical and business consultants until 1998.

Bettina Malle ▼

Malle and Schmickl believe it should be possible for everyone to produce exquisite spirits with fruits and herbs right from the garden. In 1998, they developed their first still, designed to maximize the flavor of alcoholic distillates. That same year, they launched their first webpage and online store and began to host small-scale distilling workshops. They published the results and conclusions of their experiments as well as detailed instructions and many recipes for crafting distilled spirits in their 2003 book *Schnapsbrennen als Hobby* (*The Artisan's Guide to Crafting Distilled Spirits*). It became the standard reference book for home distillers in German-spoken countries and is now in its tenth edition.

About the Authors

In the meantime they designed and constructed an optimized still for producing essential oils and hydrosols on a small scale. Due to its special designed condenser and adapted shape, the still makes it possible to obtain plenty of oil and intense hydrosols with only small amounts of base material. The two have hosted essential oil workshops and an online store since 2002 and published the reference book *Ätherische Öle selbst herstellen* (*The Essential Oils Maker's Handbook*) in 2005. The book is now in its sixth edition, and Malle and Schmickl's still is the preferred device among small-scale users in the fields of phyto-aromatherapy and herbology throughout the German-speaking region. It is widely used in many other courses, workshops, and seminaries as well as in research institutes, universities, colleges, and other educational services.

▲ Helge Schmickl

In 2008 Schmickl and Malle engineered and constructed a small-scale, modified vinegar generator that is a fixed-bed reactor with immobilized vinegar bacteria. The construction enables the use of miscellaneous packing materials, especially fruit, herbs, and spices, to improve or change the taste of the resulting vinegar. Additionally they developed a method to analyze the residual alcohol content in vinegar, which is simple, cheap, and accurate enough to determine a concentration of 0.1 percent. Their book *Essig herstellen als Hobby* (*The Artisanal Vinegar Maker's Handbook*) was published in 2010, and they have hosted vinegar workshops as well as their vinegar webpage and online store since 2011.

Bettina and Helge have been married since 2002. That same year they moved to Klagenfurt, Carinthia (Austria), where they host their seminars and conduct research and developments in fermenting and distilling. They have two children.

Also by the authors...

The Artisanal Vinegar Maker's Handbook

by Bettina Malle and Helge Schmickl; translated by Paul Lehmann

Vinegar making is a very ancient craft. Mankind first harnessed the creation of vinegar, along with its preservative and medicinal qualities, more than ten thousand years ago. Nowadays, however, most guides to making your own vinegar are limited to allowing wine to ferment on its own, often with less-than-stellar results. Truly high-quality vinegar production is an art and science in itself. Austrian distillers Helge Schmickl and Bettina Malle use their experience and scientific background to provide special insight into the creation of artisanal vinegars. Detailed, step-by-step instructions for over a hundred recipes illuminate this fascinating process for beginners, and even experienced vinegar crafters are bound to refine their techniques. *ISBN 978-1-943015-02-3. Hardcover, 192 pages.*

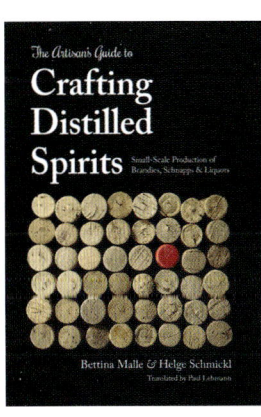

The Artisan's Guide to Crafting Distilled Spirits

by Bettina Malle and Helge Schmickl; translated by Paul Lehmann

The art of crafting alcohol is a very ancient one, and small, artisan distilleries are growing in popularity every day. Expert Austrian distillers Helge Schmickl and Bettina Malle guide readers through the process of creating or purchasing their own still and provide detailed instructions from personal experience on mash creation, fermentation, distillation, and infusion using a variety of ingredients. Schmickl and Malle also introduce readers to the tradition of schnapps distillation and present a brief look at domestic and international brewing cultures. With ninety recipes—from classic fruit brandy to chili infusions—this book is not only for the curious beginner. Even experienced distillers will discover new approaches to this classic practice. *ISBN 978-1-943015-04-7. Hardcover, 160 pages.*

www.spikehornpress.com